AQA STUDY G

GCSE 9-1
POWER AND CONFLICT

POETRY ANTHOLOGY

SCHOLASTIC

Author Richard Durant and Cindy Torn

Reviewer Rob Pollard

Editorial team Rachel Morgan, Audrey Stokes, Lesley Densham, Kate Pedlar

Typesetting Jayne Rawlings/Oxford Raw Design

Cover design Dipa Mistry and Jason Cox

App development Hannah Barnett, Phil Crothers and RAIOSOFT International Pvt Ltd

Photographs

page 11 and 12: Ramses statue feet, BMPix/iStock; page 15: Victorian London, duncan1890/iStock; page 16: manacles, Moussa81/iStock; chimney sweep, Denise LeBlanc/Shutterstock; page 20: Lake District, Rob Barklamb/Shutterstock; page 21: rowing boat, canadastock/Shutterstock; page 22: oar, Greg Mann/Shutterstock; night sky, Zacarias Pereira da Mata/Shutterstock; page 23: Buttermere, Undivided/Shutterstock; page 26: portrait of a lady by Titian, Everett – Art/Shutterstock; gold coins from Italy, 1500s, DrGrounds/iStock; page 27 and 29: COSINO I DE\x90 MEDICI, by Workshop of Bronzino, Everett – Art/Shutterstock; page 28: scroll, Andris Tkacenko/Shutterstock; page 32: Charge of the Light Brigade, duncan1890/iStock; page 33: cannon, fifty2d/Shutterstock; page 34: detail from *The Relief of the Light Brigade* by Richard Caton Woodville, National Army Museum; page 38: barbed wire, ovbelov/iStock; page 38 and 40: soldiers, © 2019 Military Machine; page 39: pickaxe and shovel, rawf8/Shutterstock; page 43: Atlantic waves, greenphotoKK/Shutterstock; page 44: house on coast of Ireland, Markus Gann/Shutterstock; sea crashing on coast, Teerasak Chinnasot/Shutterstock; page 47: soldier, breakermaximus/Shutterstock; wild hare running, Volodymyr Burdiak/Shutterstock; page 48: bullets hitting earth, Alexander Oganezov/Shutterstock; page 51: Yemen, anasalhajj/Shutterstock; page 52: soldier, Olena Yakobchuk/Shutterstock; page 55: poppy, Ed Samuel/Shutterstock; poppy field, Nitr/Shutterstock; page 56: war memorial, Kevin J. Frost/Shutterstock; page 57: white dove, Sanit Fuangnakhon/Shutterstock; page 59: photographer, Corepics VOF/Shutterstock; page 60: film roll, Chamille White/Shutterstock; page 64: Muslim woman reading Koran, ozgurkeser/iStock; receipts, peepo/iStock; page 65: tissue paper, TayaCho/iStock; skin, flubydust/iStock; page 66 and 69: sunrise, Paul Orr/Shutterstock; page 69: Mostar's Stari Most, Maelick/Shutterstock; page 70: doll, trigga/iStock; page 74: Nanny of the Maroons, Janusz Pienkowski/Shutterstock; page 75: Toussaint L'Ouverture, Everett Historical/Shutterstock; page 76: palm tree, DNY59/iStock; page 77: Shaka memorial, meunierd/Shutterstock; page 80: man, Glowonconcept/Shutterstock; page 81: Japanese fighter plane, Keith Tarrier/Shutterstock; page 82: large tuna, J'nel/Shutterstock; page 92: girl sitting exam, Monkey Business Images/Shutterstock

Published in the UK by Scholastic Education, 2019
Book End, Range Road, Witney, Oxfordshire, OX29 0YD
Scholastic Ireland, 89E Lagan Road, Dublin Industrial Estate, Glasnevin, Dublin, D11 HP5F

SCHOLASTIC and associated logos are trademarks and/or registered trademarks of Scholastic Inc.

www.scholastic.co.uk
© 2019 Scholastic Limited

4 5 6 7 8 9 1 2 3 4 5 6 7 8 9 0

A CIP catalogue record for this book is available from the British Library.
ISBN 978-1407-18321-3

Printed by Bell and Bain
Paper made from wood grown in sustainable forests and other controlled sources.

Designed using Adobe InDesign

Acknowledgements

The publishers gratefully acknowledge permission to reproduce the following copyright material: **Bloodaxe Books** for 'Tissue' by Imtiaz Dharker from *The terrorist at my table* by Imtiaz Dharker, (Bloodaxe Books, 2006); **John Agard c/o Caroline Sheldon Literary Agency Ltd** for 'Checking Out Me History' by John Agard (1996); **Carol Rumens** for 'The Emigrée' by Carol Rumens from *Thinking of Skins* by Carol Rumens (Bloodaxe Books, 1993); **Faber & Faber** for 'Bayonet Charge' by Ted Hughes from *Collected Poems* by Ted Hughes, (Faber & Faber, 2005) and for 'Storm on the Island' by Seamus Heaney from *Opened Ground* by Seamus Heaney, (Faber & Faber, 2001); **Carol Ann Duffy c/o Rogers, Coleridge & White Ltd** for 'War Photographer' from *Standing Female Nude* by Carol Ann Duffy, (Anvil Press Poetry, 1985); **Pomona** for 'Remains' by Simon Armitage from *The Not Dead* by Simon Armitage, (Pomona Press, 2008); **Templar Poetry** for 'Poppies' by Jane Weir from *The way I dressed during the revolution* edited by Alexander McMillen, (Templar Poetry, 2010) and for 'Kamikaze' by Beatrice Garland from *The Invention of Fireworks* edited by Alexander McMillen, (Templar Poetry, 2013); **Guardian News & Media Ltd** for quotation from 'Imtiaz Dharker awarded Queen's gold medal for poetry' article by Mark Brown, (*The Guardian*, 2014)

Every effort has been made to trace copyright holders for the works reproduced in this book, and the publishers apologise for any inadvertent omissions.

Note from the publisher:
Please use this product in conjunction with the official specification and sample assessment materials. Ask your teacher if you are unsure where to find them.

Contents

Check your answers on the free revision app or at www.scholastic.co.uk/gcse

How to use this book

This Study Guide is designed to help you prepare effectively for your AQA GCSE English literature exam question on Poetry anthology – Cluster 2: Power and conflict (Paper 2, Section B).

The content has been organised to allow you to work through the whole of cluster 2 step by step, one poem at a time. You can choose the order in which you would like to study the poems. However, you should ensure that you work through *all* of the content in the book. This will build confidence and deepen your knowledge and understanding of all the poems.

HOW TO REVISE!

Know the poems

1 It is very important that you know the poems well. Read and study them. Make up your own mind about them. The poems in this Study Guide are set out on the page with every five lines marked for ease of reference. Some words and phrases are underlined for analysis within the guide. Add your own annotations to the poem, exploring more of its details and their effects. Choose details for yourself but do also include the underlined words or phrases. You might like to do your annotations after you have read the full analysis of each poem as outlined in step 2.

Cluster 2: Power and conflict

2 The **Cluster 2: Power and conflict** section on pages 10–83 takes you through the anthology poems one at a time. They provide analysis of themes, contexts, language, structure and form of every poem.

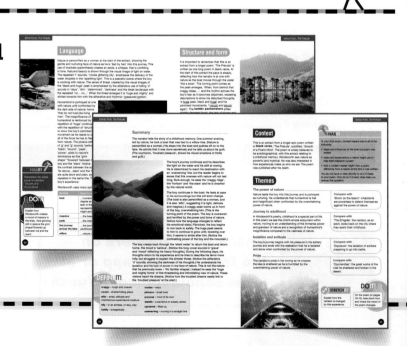

Essentials

3 At the end of the poems section, you will find essential information on pages 84 and 85 which focuses on the overarching themes and sub-themes in the Cluster.

This section will help you understand how to write a good answer to the question in Section B. Additional activities are provided for you to work through and practise.

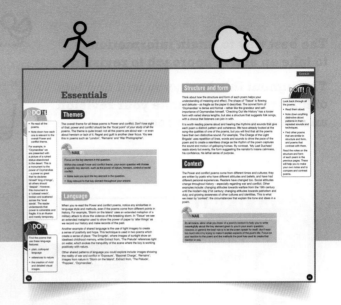

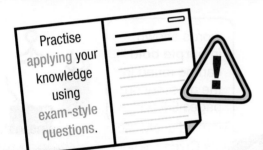

Practise applying your knowledge using exam-style questions.

Doing well in your AQA exam

4 Finally, you will find an extended 'Doing well in your AQA exam' section which guides you through the process of understanding questions, and planning and writing answers.

Stick to the **TIME LIMITS** you will need to in the exam.

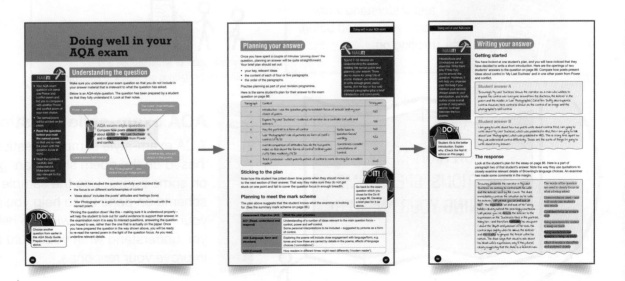

Features of this guide

The best way to retain information is to take an active approach to revision.

Throughout this book, you will find lots of features that will make your revision an active, successful process.

SNAPIT!

Use the Snap it! feature in the revision app to take pictures of key concepts and information. Great for revision on the go!

DEFINEIT!

Explains the meaning of difficult words from the poems.

Callouts Additional explanations of important points.

Regular exercise helps stimulate the brain and will help you relax.

words shown in **purple bold** can be found in the glossary on pages 94–95

Find methods of relaxation that work for you throughout the revision period.

DOIT!

Activities to embed your knowledge and understanding and prepare you for the exam.

NAILIT!

Succinct and vital tips on how to do well in your exam.

STRETCHIT!

Provides content that stretches you further.

REVIEWIT!

Helps you to consolidate and understand what you have learned before moving on.

Revise in pairs or small groups and deliver presentations on topics to each other.

AQA exam-style question

AQA exam-style sample questions based on the poem shown are given on some pages. Use the sample mark scheme on page 88 to help you assess your responses. This will also help you understand what you could do to improve your response.

FOR HIGH-MARK QUESTIONS, SPEND TIME **PLANNING** YOUR ANSWER!

FREE REVISION APP

- The **free revision app** can be downloaded to your mobile phone (iOS and Android), making **on-the go-revision** easy.

- Use the revision calendar to help map out your revision in the lead-up to the exam.

- Complete multiple-choice questions and create your own SNAP**IT!** revision cards.

www.scholastic.co.uk/gcse

Online answers and additional resources

All of the tasks in this book are designed to get you thinking and to consolidate your understanding through thought and application. Therefore, it is important to write your own answers before checking. Use a separate piece of paper so that you can draft your response and work out the best way of answering.

Online you will find a copy of each poem with detailed annotations. Do not look at those until you have explored the poem thoroughly for yourself.

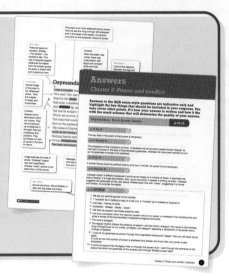

Get plenty of sleep, especially the night before an exam.

LOOK AFTER YOURSELF

Help your brain by looking after your whole body!

Once you have worked through a section, you can check your answers to Do it!, Stretch it!, Review it! and the exam practice sections on the app or at **www.scholastic.co.uk/gcse**. Annotated poems are available at **www.scholastic.co.uk/gcse-poetry**.

Why study Power and conflict poetry?

Even before you read your collection of poetry, you will have considered how people seek power and cause conflict in a number of ways in our lives. Conflict is not a modern invention, it has been written about, depicted through art and sung about throughout our history. This cluster of poems, Power and conflict, gives us an overview of how poets have viewed our quest for power from 1817 to the present day. The 'conflict' in these poems isn't just about war and fighting, nor is 'power' about politicians and royalty. We are shown the grim reality of war; we are shown conflict's impact on our lives long after the conflict is over; we are shown the pain of finding our identity in the world.

What is the aim of the Power and conflict collection?

The aim of the collection is to show us how we react to power and conflict unifies us across history. If we wish to grow as people who can learn from the pain and suffering that others have been through, through a whole range of situations, we can learn from the varied experiences these poets bring us.

Power and conflict poetry in your AQA exam

Power and conflict is examined in Section B (the second section) of the second AQA GCSE English Literature exam, Paper 2 Modern Texts and Poetry. Here is how it fits into the overall assessment framework:

Paper 1 Time: **1 hour 45 minutes**	Paper 2 Time: **2 hours 15 minutes**
Section A: Shakespeare	Section A: Modern prose or drama
Section B: 19th-century novel	**Section B: Poetry anthology Cluster 2: Power and conflict**
	Section C: Unseen poetry

There will be just one question on the Power and conflict cluster and you should not answer questions on any other cluster (e.g. 'Love and relationships'). Only answer the Power and conflict question. You should spend **40 minutes** planning and writing your answer to the question. There are 30 marks available for the Power and conflict question.

The Power and conflict question will come with a copy of the selected poem from the cluster printed on your exam paper. You will find the question just before the poem. The question will ask you to compare a theme from the given poem with one other poem of your choice from the Power and conflict cluster. You must answer the question in relation to the printed poem and to one other poem that you have chosen for yourself.

NAILIT!

- Keep a close watch on the time in your exam. Don't spend more than 45 minutes on the modern prose or drama question or you will have less time to write your answer to the Power and conflict question in Section B (40 minutes) or the unseen question in Section C (50 minutes).

Poems organised by theme

Power/tyranny
My Last Duchess
Ozymandias
The Emigrée

War/conflict
Bayonet Charge
The Charge of the Light Brigade
Exposure
Poppies
Remains
War Photographer

Social conflict
Checking Out Me History
Kamikaze
London
The Emigrée
Tissue
War Photographer

Inner conflict
Kamikaze
Remains
War Photographer

The reality of war
Bayonet Charge
Exposure
Remains
War Photographer

Loss/absence
My Last Duchess
Poppies
The Emigrée

Power of nature
Bayonet Charge
Extract from, The Prelude
Exposure
Storm on the Island

Identity
The Emigrée
Checking Out Me History
Tissue
Storm on the Island
War Photographer

Inequality
London
War Photographer

Obedience and duty
Bayonet Charge
The Charge of the Light Brigade
Kamikaze
My Last Duchess

Regret/guilt
London
Kamikaze
Extract from, The Prelude
Remains
War Photographer

Suffering/misery
Exposure
London
Poppies
Remains
War Photographer

Control
My Last Duchess
War Photographer

Heroism/or lack of
The Charge of the Light Brigade
Bayonet Charge
Exposure
Remains

DO IT!

For each theme, choose two poems that are relevant to the theme but have contrasting points of view. For example:

'Exposure' and 'The Charge of the Light Brigade'. In both poems, we see a contrasting view of war. This war is fought heroically by 'noble' troops in 'The Charge of the Light Brigade' whereas we are shown a dark view of a war in 'Exposure' with troops facing the monotony of waiting and dying from cold.

Ozymandias

Percy Bysshe Shelley (1792–1822)

I <u>met a traveller</u> from an antique land
Who said: Two vast and trunkless legs of stone
Stand in the desert. Near them on the sand,
Half sunk, a shattered visage lies, whose frown
5   And wrinkled lip, and sneer of cold command
Tell that its sculptor well those passions read
Which yet survive, stamped on these lifeless things,
The hand that mocked them and the heart that fed;
And on the pedestal these words appear:
10   'My name is Ozymandias, king of kings:
<u>Look on my works, ye Mighty, and despair!'</u>
Nothing beside remains. Round the decay
Of that colossal wreck, boundless and bare,
The lone and level sands stretch far away.

Summary

The **narrator** tells us that he met a traveller who told him about two huge legs of a statue standing in the desert. (Notice the use of reported speech here. This distances the reader from the story giving a dream-like, mysterious quality to the poem.) Nearby, there's the broken head of the statue. He describes the expressions on the face showing a 'sneer' and 'cold command' (these expressions suggest a tyrannical ruler). The narrator remarks that the sculptor must have seen these expressions to create them, and they survive on the broken statue's face. (Notice the word-play on 'mocked'; as an artist you 'mock up' a sculpture but mock also means to make fun of.)

There is an inscription on the broken statue that gives his name, 'Ozymandias', this reveals that he thought he was the greatest ruler, 'king of kings' and then states that powerful rulers should look at his achievements and 'despair' at their own. (Notice the irony: he is saying that they must be unhappy about their own power and achievements, while his power and achievements have crumbled into dust and no one is listening!)

We are told that nothing else remains, either of the statue or the civilisation that created it. The sands stretch all around the 'wreck' – the broken statue. (Remember that sand is often used as a symbol for the passing of time.)

DO IT!

What point do you think Shelley is making in this poem?

STRETCH IT!

Explain how Shelley uses irony to emphasise his key point.

Context

When Shelley was writing the poem, Egypt and the ancient world was a fashionable subject. Shelley was radical in his political thinking, and in this poem we see his political message that power is temporary and will crumble into dust just like this 'colossal wreck'.

Themes

Power

The poem presents power as temporary. The irony at the heart of the poem is that all of Ozymandias's power is reduced to dust: there is no one to hear (or care about) his declaration of his power in the desert.

Compare with
'Tissue': this poem uses paper to represent the fragile nature of life as we know it.

Nature

The power of nature over humankind is shown through the 'level sands' that consume the statue, which symbolises the power and achievements of humankind.

Compare with
Extract from, 'The Prelude': this poem also explores humankind's fragility in the face of nature.

Time

The poem shows us that even mighty kings will be forgotten in the sands of time. Nothing will remain of their legacy other than a 'colossal wreck'.

Compare with
'Poppies': time gradually erases the memory of the woman's dead son; 'inscriptions on the war memorial'.

Pride

Pride (or hubris – meaning excessive pride or self-confidence) is explored through the arrogant tone of the inscription on the broken statue. The irony that this 'colossal wreck' is all that is left of the ruler's achievements emphasises the key message that power is temporary.

Compare with
'My Last Duchess': the duke's self-pride makes him determined to control his wife, even by murdering her.

DOIT!

What other themes can you find in the poem? Briefly explain one additional theme that is relevant to both 'Ozymandias' and Power and conflict.

Language

The central image of the poem is the 'shattered' statue in the desert. This statue, representing the power of the ruler – now a 'colossal wreck' – symbolises the futility of humankind's pursuit of power. The 'vast' nature of the statue represents his arrogant self-perceptions. He sees himself as 'king of kings' – the best of the best. Here the language of 'decay' – 'shattered' 'wreck' – is juxtaposed with the proud and arrogant tone of the inscription: 'Look on my works, ye Mighty, and despair!'

STRETCHIT!

Explain why the image 'colossal wreck' is effective.

The cruelty of the ruler is reinforced by the **alliteration** of harsh sounds 'cold command'. The power of nature is expressed in the bludgeoning alliteration of 'boundless and bare'. Notice that the sculptor was able to 'read' those expressions and reproduce them. Here we have another set of images relating to the power of art. The ruler is gone and forgotten, but in the sculptor's work, these 'passions' live on.

Structure and form

The poem is written as a sonnet – a 14-line poem. This tight **structure** is perfect for summing up some big ideas relating to time; the fragility of power and humankind's powerlessness in the face of nature.

Shelley presents a range of voices and speakers in the poem. We have a narrator who is retelling the traveller's story as well as the voice of Ozymandias himself through the inscription on the pedestal.

REVIEW IT!

1 Is the traveller male or female?

2 What two meanings of the word 'mocked' does Shelley use?

3 What does Shelley mean by 'trunkless'?

4 Find two examples of the language of decay.

5 Find a quotation to show that the sculptor was good at his/her job.

6 What effect does the use of reported speech have on the reader?

7 What is the tone of the inscription on the ruined statue?

8 Give one reason for Shelley's use of **rhythm** in the poem.

9 Explain the two meanings of the line: 'Look on my works, ye Mighty, and despair!'

10 Although the ruler is forgotten and his 'mighty works' have vanished or been broken, how could you argue that his legacy lives on?

DO IT!

- Add your own annotations to the poem, exploring more of its details and their **effects**. Include the underlined words or phrases.

- Online you will find a copy of the poem with more detailed annotations.

AQA exam-style question

Compare how poets present the temporary nature of power in 'Ozymandias' and in one other poem from Power and conflict.

[30 marks]

London

William Blake (1757–1827)

I wander through each <u>chartered</u> street,
Near where the chartered Thames does flow,
And <u>mark</u> in every face I meet
<u>Marks</u> of weakness, <u>marks</u> of woe.

5   In <u>every</u> cry of every <u>man</u>,
In <u>every</u> infant's cry of <u>fear</u>,
In <u>every</u> voice, in every <u>ban</u>,
The <u>mind-forged manacles</u> I <u>hear</u>:

How the chimney-sweeper's cry
10 Every <u>black'ning</u> church appalls,
And the haple<u>ss</u> <u>s</u>oldier'<u>s</u> <u>s</u>igh
Runs in blood down <u>palace</u> walls.

But most through midnight streets I hear
How the <u>youthful harlot's curse</u>
15 <u>Blasts</u> the new-born infant's tear,
And <u>blights</u> with plagues the <u>marriage hearse</u>.

Summary

The narrator says he wanders through London's streets and notices the exhaustion, illness and unhappiness in the faces around him. (The repeated word 'chartered' is significant: Blake emphasises that the people own nothing and have no control over their own lives; Blake implies that they too are 'chartered'.)

The narrator hears unhappiness and fear in the voices around him. He realises that the ordinary citizens are controlled by their despair, which has been created by their oppressors. (Their control is 'mind-forged', suggesting that they are controlled through mental rather than physical means.)

The narrator draws attention to features of city life that the church and the government should be ashamed of: child chimney sweeps and abandoned disabled soldiers. (Note Blake's **allusions** to child labour and the neglect of ex-servicemen who have given their 'blood' for king and country.)

Most of all, the narrator notes the swearing of young prostitutes and is appalled to think of how the diseases they spread to their clients' families 'blight' marriages and infect children as they are born. (Through the hard 'bl-' alliterations and the shocking 'marriage hearse' image, Blake forcefully expresses his dismay with life in London for most people.)

Context

Blake was writing at the time of the industrial revolution, when city populations suddenly increased. People were packed into the growing cities, where they had to work long hours in the factories whose smoke polluted the air. Blake was angered by the destruction of the natural environment, and by the callousness and greed of the powerful few who owned and controlled almost everything. Blake was a Christian but he did not support the organised Churches.

DEFINE IT!

appalls – shock and horrify

ban – prohibition; (also echoes of **bann** – announcement of a wedding)

blights – ruins, infects

chartered – privately owned

forged – shaped through heat and deliberate force

hapless – unlucky

harlot – prostitute

hearse – cart for carrying a body to a funeral

manacles – metal cuffs used to control a prisoner

woe – unhappiness

DO IT!

Choose five quotations and explain how they link to the **contextual** information above.

Themes

Power

The people are forced to work until they are exhausted and ill. They are controlled by 'mind-forged manacles'. The ordinary people own nothing: the rich and powerful own even the public spaces and resources (for example, the streets and the river).

> **Compare with**
> 'Ozymandias': rulers lose their power eventually despite their 'sneer of cold command'.
>
> 'My Last Duchess'

Suffering and misery

The people all have expressions of 'woe'. Men 'cry', babies are frightened, soldiers are unlucky and ignored despite their injuries, and the population is 'blighted' with sexually transmitted diseases (STDs) that raise infant mortality.

> **Compare with**
> 'Exposure': here there is more physical suffering: 'Our brains ache'; 'winds that knive us'.

Injustice

The word 'chartered' was a late choice. Blake had originally written 'dirty'. 'Chartered' shifts the poem's focus from urban misery to the inequality that causes it. Meanwhile those who have responsibility for their people – the government and the Church – seem to not care about their poverty and misery.

> **Compare with**
> 'War Photographer': here people in general seem not to care ('they do not care').

DO IT!

Choose two of the three themes explored on this page.

For each theme, list one more poem that you could compare with 'London'.

Briefly explain each choice.

Language

Blake expresses complex ideas through the use of compressed and very powerful **metaphors**: for example, the **oxymoron** of the 'marriage hearse' image confronts the reader with conflicting ideas: 'marriage' (happiness) and 'hearse' (grief). The effect is immediate and shocking.

Blake affects the reader directly through other means. **Sibilance** emphasises the sighing of the soldiers, and the blunt alliteration of 'blasts' and 'blights' conveys the violence being done to the ordinary people of London by the urban chaos and poverty.

STRETCH IT!

Explain the phrase 'black'ning church' and how it contributes to the poem's meaning.

Structure and form

The poem has a regular rhythm and **rhyme** scheme. Most of its lines are **iambic** tetrameters. That means they have (mostly) eight syllables and four **stresses**, alternating between unstressed and stressed syllables. For example:

> In <u>every</u> <u>cry</u> of <u>every</u> <u>man</u>...

Because iambic lines stress the final syllable, the rhymes are strengthened.

The even rhythm and rhymes and the repeated words in the first two **stanzas** give the poem an insistent, ominous feel that suits its bleak content and leads the reader towards the final, shocking 'marriage hearse' image.

See how this student makes a connection between the poem's structure and its meaning:

The poem's irresistible movement seems to control the reader, just as the London poor are controlled by their powerful masters.

The four stanzas are arranged for logical and dramatic effect, and this gives the poem added 'punch':

Stanza	Key ideas
1	Appalling sights
2	Appalling sounds
3	Shame and blame
4	Appalling results

REVIEW IT!

1 In what sense are the streets and the river 'chartered'?

2 What two different meanings of the word 'mark' does Blake use?

3 What does the narrator hear in the crying of babies?

4 What does Blake mean by 'manacles'?

5 In what two senses are the churches 'blackened'?

6 Explain a possible cause for the 'soldier's sigh'.

7 What 'blasts the new-born infant's tear'?

8 What might Blake mean by 'marriage hearse'?

9 How many syllables are in an iambic tetrameter, and how many of them are stressed when read aloud?

10 Why do you think Blake called his poem 'London' rather than choosing a title based on ideas in the poem?

DO IT!

AQA exam-style question

Compare how poets present suffering in 'London' and in one other poem from Power and conflict.

[30 marks]

- Add your own annotations to the poem, exploring more of its details and their effects. Include the underlined words or phrases.

- Online you will find a copy of the poem with more detailed annotations.

Extract from, The Prelude
William Wordsworth (1770–1850)

One summer evening (led by her) I found
A little boat tied to a willow tree
Within a rocky cove, its usual home.
Straight I unloosed her chain, and stepping in
5   Pushed from the shore. It was an act of stealth
And troubled pleasure, nor without the voice
Of mountain-echoes did my boat move on;
Leaving behind her still, on either side,
Small circles glittering idly in the moon,
10 Until they melted all into one track
Of sparkling light. But now, like one who rows,
Proud of his skill, to reach a chosen point
With an unswerving line, I fixed my view
Upon the summit of a craggy ridge,
15 The horizon's utmost boundary; far above
Was nothing but the stars and the grey sky.
She was an elfin pinnace; lustily
I dipped my oars into the silent lake,
And, as I rose upon the stroke, my boat
20 Went heaving through the water like a swan;
When, from behind that craggy steep till then
The horizon's bound, a huge peak, black and huge,
As if with voluntary power instinct,
Upreared its head. I struck and struck again,
25 And growing still in stature the grim shape
Towered up between me and the stars, and still,
For so it seemed, with purpose of its own
And measured motion like a living thing,
Strode after me. With trembling oars I turned,
30 And through the silent water stole my way
Back to the covert of the willow tree;
There in her mooring-place I left my bark, -
And through the meadows homeward went, in grave
And serious mood; but after I had seen
35 That spectacle, for many days, my brain

Worked with a dim and undetermined sense
Of unknown modes of being; o'er my thoughts
There hung a darkness, call it solitude
Or blank desertion. No familiar shapes
40 Remained, no pleasant images of trees,
Of sea or sky, no colours of green fields;
But huge and mighty forms, that do not live
Like living men, moved slowly through the mind
By day, and were a trouble to my dreams.

Summary

The narrator tells the story of a childhood memory. One summer evening, led by nature, he took a boat that was tied to a willow tree. (Nature is personified as a woman.) He steps into the boat and pushes off on to the lake. He admits that it was done secretively and he tells us about his guilt. (The oxymoron, 'troubled pleasure', shows his mixed emotions of thrills and guilt.)

The boy's journey continues and he describes the light on the water and his skill at rowing. He is determined to reach his destination with an 'unswerving' line, but the reader begins to sense that this oneness with nature will not last long. Sure enough, he sees the 'craggy ridge', the 'horizon' and 'the stars' and he is dwarfed by the natural world.

The boy continues in the boat. He feels at ease in his surroundings but this will soon change. (The boat is also personified as a woman, and it is also 'elfin', suggesting it is light, delicate and magical.) A craggy peak looms up in front of the boy, overwhelming him. (This is the turning point of the poem. The boy is overawed and terrified by the power and force of nature. Notice how the language changes to reflect his emotional state.) Panicked, the boy begins to row back to safety. The huge peak seems to him to continue to grow until, towering over him, it seems to stride after him. (Notice the contrasting power of the boy and the mountain.)

The boy creeps back through the 'silent water' to return the boat and return home. His mood is 'serious'. (Notice the long vowel sounds in 'grave' and 'mood' reflecting his heavy thoughts.) During the following days, his thoughts return to his experience and he tries to describe his terror more fully, but struggles to explain the sinister threat. (Notice the alliterative 'd' sounds, showing the darkness of his thoughts.) He understands his isolation and his lack of power in the face of nature. This is not the nature that he previously knew – 'No familiar shapes'; instead he sees the 'huge and mighty forms' of this threatening and intimidating view of nature. These visions haunt his dreams. (Notice how the troubled dreams neatly link to the 'troubled pleasure' at the start.)

DEFINE IT!

craggy – rough and uneven	**modes** – ways
covert – shelter/hiding place	**pinnace** – small boat
elfin – small, delicate and mischievous supernatural creature	**purpose** – mind of its own
idly – in an aimless, or lazy, way	**stealth** – a secretive or sneaky action
lustily – energetically	**upreared** – lifted up
	unswerving – moving in a straight line

Context

This is an extract from a longer epic poem written in **blank verse**, 'The Prelude', subtitled, 'Growth of a Poet's Mind'. The poem is widely believed to be autobiographical, with this extract relating to a childhood memory. Wordsworth saw nature as powerful and mystical. He was also interested in how experiences make us who we are. The poem was published after his death.

NAILIT!

In your AQA exam, context means one or all of the following:

- ideas and influences at the time the poem was written
- ideas and expectations a reader might use to help them interpret a poem
- how a modern reader might view a poem differently from a reader at the time it was written.

You do not *have* to refer directly to any of these in your exam. Only do so if it really does help you answer the question.

Themes

The power of nature

Nature leads the boy into this journey and is portrayed as nurturing. He understands that humankind is frail and insignificant when confronted by the overwhelming power of nature.

Compare with
'Storm on the Island': inhabitants are powerless to defend themselves against the power of nature.

Journey to adulthood

In Wordsworth's poetry, childhood is a special part of life. In this poem we see the child's simple enjoyment within nature, moving to an understanding of the immense power and grandeur of nature and a recognition of humankind's insignificance compared to the vastness of nature.

Compare with
'The Emigrée': the narrator, as an adult, looks back on the city where they spent their childhood.

Isolation and solitude

The boy's journey begins with his pleasure in his solitary journey and ends with the realisation that he is isolated and alone when confronted by the power of nature.

Compare with
'Exposure': the isolation of soldiers preparing to go into battle.

Pride

The narrator's pride in his rowing as he crosses the lake is shattered as he is humbled by the overwhelming power of nature.

Compare with
'Ozymandias': the great works of the ruler lie shattered and broken in the desert.

 STRETCHIT!

Explain how the narrator is changed by this experience.

 DOIT!

On the poem on pages 18–19, note down how and where the mood of the poem changes.

Language

Nature is personified as a woman at the start of the extract, showing the gentle and nurturing face of nature as he is '(led by her)' into this journey. This use of brackets (parenthesis) creates an aside, a whisper, that is confiding in tone. Nature's beauty is shown through the visual image of light on water. The repeated 'l' sounds, 'circles glittering idly', emphasise the delicacy of the water droplets in the 'sparkling light'. This is a peaceful scene where the boy is working with nature. The sense of threat, created by the visual images of the 'black and huge' peak is emphasised by the alliterative use of tolling 'd' sounds in 'days', 'dim', 'determined', 'darkness' and the bleak landscape with the repeated 'no... no...' When the threat emerges it is 'huge and mighty' and strides towards him with the alliterative and rhythmic 'measured motion'.

Humankind is portrayed at one with nature until confronted by the dark side of nature; forms 'that do not live/Like living men'. The insignificance of humankind is reinforced by the repetition of 'huge' continued with the repetition of 'struck' to show the boy's panicked movement as he needs to use all of the force he has to flee from nature. The plosive string of 'p' and 'b' sounds 'behind', 'black', 'bound', 'peak', 'power', adds to nature's dominance as this 'grim shape' 'Towered' between the boy and the 'stars'. Notice

the contrast between the scared and panicked boy and the vastness of the 'far above...stars' and the 'huge' peak. Here, Wordsworth's language choices are quite blunt and plain, even clumsy: 'upreared', 'towered up' and 'huge' repeated in the same line. These choices reinforce the physical threat to the boy's experience.

Wordsworth uses many symbols and images to convey his meanings:

Symbol	Used to show...
boat	...humankind's ability to survive and get along with nature to a degree as it enables the boy to travel over the water; however, later in the poem, we are shown the boat's delicacy, perhaps representing humankind's fragility, when confronted by the full might and power of nature.
meadow	...the beautiful and gentle face of nature.
peak	...the menacing and overwhelming power of nature.
the journey across the lake	...the journey from innocence to experience, childhood to adulthood.
willow	...nature; notice that the boat is 'tied' to nature.

NAILIT!

Remember the whole poem is subtitled, 'Growth of a Poet's Mind'.

DOIT!

Explain how Wordsworth creates a mood of menace in the lines, 'And growing still in stature the grim shape/Towered up between me and the stars'.

Structure and form

It is important to remember that this is an extract from a longer poem. 'The Prelude' is written as one long poem in blank verse. At the start of this extract the pace is steady, reflecting how the narrator is at one with nature as the boat moves through the water 'like a swan'. The turning point comes as the peak emerges, 'When, from behind that craggy steep…', and the rhythm echoes the boy's fear as it becomes disjointed, repeating descriptions to show his disturbed thoughts, 'a <u>huge</u> peak, black and <u>huge</u>' and his panicked movements, 'I <u>struck</u> and <u>struck</u> again'. The **iambic pentameters** (often slightly departed from), the lack of rhyme and the **enjambments** work together to create structure necessary to sustain a narrative, but also to create irregularities that suggest private and intense thoughts and doubts.

REVIEW IT!

1 At what time of year is the poem set?

2 Where does the boy find the boat?

3 What is an 'elfin pinnace'?

4 Who leads the boy to the boat?

5 What skill is the boy proud of?

6 What **simile** is used to describe the boat's movement through the water?

7 How do we know that the boy is panicked by the peak? Find two quotations that show his panic.

8 How does nature appear to the boy after fleeing the peak?

9 Explain how this experience affects the boy.

10 What type of power or conflict is explored in this poem?

DO IT!

- Add your own annotations to the poem, exploring more of its details and their effects. Include the underlined words or phrases.

- Online you will find a copy of the poem with more detailed annotations.

AQA exam-style question

Compare how poets present ideas about a journey in the Extract from, 'The Prelude' and in one other poem from Power and conflict.

[30 marks]

My Last Duchess
Robert Browning (1812–1889)

Ferrara

That's my last Duchess painted on the <u>wall</u>,
Looking as if she were alive. I <u>call</u>
That piece a wonder, now: Frà Pandolf's <u>hands</u>
Worked busily a day, and there she <u>stands</u>.
5 <u>Will't please you</u> sit and look at her? I said
'Frà Pandolf' by design, for never read
Strangers like you that pictured countenance,
The depth and passion of its earnest glance,
But to myself they turned (since <u>none puts by</u>
10 <u>The curtain I have drawn for you, but I</u>)
And seemed as they would ask me, <u>if they durst</u>,
How such a glance came there; so, not the first
Are you to turn and ask thus. Sir, 'twas not
Her husband's presence only, called that spot
15 Of joy into the Duchess' cheek: perhaps
Frà Pandolf <u>chanced to say</u> 'Her mantle laps
Over my lady's wrist too much,' or 'Paint
Must never hope to reproduce the faint
Half-flush that dies along her throat': such stuff
20 Was courtesy, she thought, and cause enough
For calling up that spot of joy. She had
A heart – <u>how shall I say?</u> – too soon made glad,
Too easily impressed; she liked whate'er
She looked on, and <u>her looks went everywhere</u>.
25 Sir, 'twas all one! My favour at her breast,
The dropping of the daylight in the West,
The bough of cherries some officious fool
Broke in the orchard for her, the white mule
She rode with round the terrace – all and each
30 Would draw from her alike the <u>approving speech</u>,
Or blush, at least. She thanked men, – good! but thanked
Somehow – <u>I know not how</u> – as if she ranked
My gift of a nine-hundred-years-old name

With anybody's gift. Who'd stoop to blame
This sort of <u>trifling</u>? Even had you skill
35   In speech – (which I have not) – to make your will
Quite clear to such an one, and say, 'Just this
Or that in you disgusts me; here you miss,
Or there exceed the mark' – and if she let
Herself be lessoned so, nor plainly set
40   Her wits to yours, forsooth, and made excuse,
– E'en then would be some stooping; and I choose
<u>Never to stoop</u>. Oh, sir, she smiled, no doubt,
Whene'er I passed her; but who passed without
Much the same smile? This grew; <u>I gave commands</u>;
45   <u>Then all smiles stopped together</u>. There she stands
<u>As if alive</u>. Will't please you rise? We'll meet
The company below, then. I repeat,
The Count your master's known munificence
Is ample warrant that no just pretence
50   Of mine for dowry <u>will be disallowed</u>;
<u>Though his fair daughter's self, as I avowed</u>
<u>At starting, is my object</u>. Nay, we'll go
Together down, sir. Notice Neptune, though,
Taming a sea-horse, thought a rarity,
55   Which Claus of Innsbruck cast in bronze for me!

Summary

The duke (probably of Ferrara in Italy) is looking for a new wife. 'The Count' has sent a representative to find out if the duke would be a suitable husband for his daughter. The duke shows the representative a portrait of his dead wife. He says that many people have been surprised by the 'depth and passion' in the portrait's 'earnest' expression. (Note that the duke says that viewers ask about his dead wife's expression 'if they durst', suggesting that the duke is a feared man.)

The duke explains that the 'spot of joy' in the face was brought on not just by his presence but also by the painter's flattery. He complains that everything made his wife smile: his presents, sunsets, cherries brought for her. He is offended that she treated every gift with equal appreciation – even the 'nine-hundred-years-old name' that he had given her by marrying her. (Clearly the duke is a vain man who demands to be the centre of attention, obeyed by everyone.)

He was unwilling to lower himself by telling her off, so he 'gave commands' – presumably for her murder. (The duke is not explicit about what he did. He lets the listener reach his own chilling conclusions.)

Now the duke suggests they join the rest of the guests. He says that although he values the count's daughter for her 'self', he will expect a large dowry. He points out a valuable bronze statue that has been specially cast for him. (The duke makes it clear that he always gets what he wants – whether that is a statue or a wife.)

DEFINE IT!

ample – enough

avowed – stated

bough – large branch

countenance – face

(by) design – deliberately

dowry – money given by the bride's family to the groom

durst – dared

favour – present (perhaps a brooch)

forsooth – indeed, in truth

just pretence – fair request

mantle – cloak

munificence – generosity

Neptune – god of the sea

officious – fussy and interfering

stoop – lower (himself)

thus – (in) that (way)

trifling – unacceptably light behaviour

'twas – it was

warrant – guarantee

whate'er – whatever

whene'er – whenever

will't – will it

Context

The poem is set in the 1500s in Italy, a country that was split into many city states ruled by dukes. These men were so powerful that they could order the murder of 'inconvenient' people. In order not to provoke a rebellion against them, dukes distanced themselves from such cold killings.

NAILIT!

Context is only relevant if it sheds light on the poems and your exam question. Look at these two students' comments on context. The first is useful: it locates the poem within the theme of the whole poetry cluster: power. The second is pointless.

Student Answer A

'My Last Duchess' gives a chilling picture of total power in the hands of a cruel and selfish tyrant.

Student Answer B

Robert Browning sets the poem in the 16th century.

Themes

Power and tyranny

The duke is a cruel tyrant who does what he likes. His power and confidence are immediately clear from his observation that visitors only question him 'if they durst'.

> **Compare with**
> Extract from, 'The Prelude': the narrator is terrified of the 'power' of the peak that looms over him.

Control

He insists on controlling his wives: he requires them to satisfy his vanity at all times and to keep their attention on him. He does not allow a wife to pit her 'wits' against him – to be an equal.

> **Compare with**
> 'War Photographer': the photographer uses pictures to control ('order') experience.

Appearance and reality

Because we only know events from the duke's own narrative, we have to 'read between the lines' to recognise his true, evil nature. The contrast between reality and appearance is summed up by the portrait, which shows the murdered duchess 'as if alive'.

> **Compare with**
> 'The Emigrée': the contrast between the city as it really is and the narrator's 'sunlight-clear' memory of it.

DOIT!

Choose two more themes relevant to 'My Last Duchess' and to Power and conflict.

For each theme, list one more poem that you could compare with 'My Last Duchess'.

Briefly explain each of your choices.

Language

Here is what one student wrote about the duke's language:

> Browning gives the narrator an often vague and rambling way of speaking. Occasionally though, sharp details in the narrative reveal the duke's true feelings: for example, his sensual description of the 'faint/Half-flush' along the duchess's throat hints at his obsessive jealousy and possessiveness. These sudden shifts from ordinary language to sharp details makes him even more threatening.

Note how the student comments on the *effect* of Browning's use of language.

The duke's choice of language is deliberately vague: he says 'this grew' without explaining precisely what he means, and that therefore he 'gave commands', again without explaining who and what he commanded. This vagueness allows the duke to threaten his listener without openly admitting his ruthlessness. His use of the **euphemism** 'trifling' in relation to his wife, when he really means 'offensive behaviour', provides a further example of his manipulative nature, and makes the listener feel uneasy about him.

Structure and form

The poem is a dramatic **monologue** delivered to one, mysterious listener. The real story of the 'last Duchess' is only hinted at, and this makes the whole monologue intriguing and sinister. Our attention is maintained by the duke's style of speaking: he sprinkles his chilling narrative with hesitations such as 'how shall I say?' and 'I know not how', but his pretend lack of confidence creates a striking contrast with the obvious reality: the duke is an all-powerful, cruel tyrant.

Browning presents the poem as one long stanza divided into **rhyming couplets** based on iambic pentameters. This controlled structure conveys the duke's own power and control. This structure could become monotonous but Browning disrupts the poem's flow with features that suit an informal speech. These disruptions mainly consist of punctuation in the middle of lines and enjambment that carries the sense of a line over its end rhyme and on to the next line.

These deliberate disruptions to the poem's flow are suited to a speech which the duke pretends he is making up as he goes along. In fact, he is carefully choosing his words and varying his pace to have the effect he desires on his listener: to control the listener just as he tried to control the duchess.

DO IT!

1 Read the poem out loud to yourself. Pay close attention to Browning's punctuation and how it signals shifts in the mood and pace of the duke's monologue.

2 Read the poem again, trying out a slightly different tone and emphasis for the duke's voice.

See how one student makes both direct and indirect references to the poem to support their ideas about its structure. An examiner has made some notes alongside.

> Because the narrator is using his story to hint his ruthlessness to the listener, the poem often changes pace and direction for dramatic effect. For example, the narrator gives the impression of being foolish and rambling when he lists his last duchess's 'crimes' and ingratitudes, but suddenly his style changes from elaborate to pithy when he reports that 'Then all smiles stopped together.'

This student uses indirect evidence to make general references to ideas in the poem and uses direct reference in the form of a quotation. Both forms of evidence are valid.

REVIEW IT!

1 Which words show that the 'last Duchess' is dead?
2 Who is allowed to draw the curtain in front of the portrait?
3 What is the name of the painter who did the last duchess's portrait?
4 What did the 'officious fool' give the duchess?
5 What does the duke say he would never do?
6 Why is the duke sure he will get a large dowry with his next wife?
7 Why did the duke resent his 'last Duchess'?
8 How does the poem's form and structure suggest the duke's power?
9 What is sinister about the duke's words?
10 What can we **infer** about the duke and his personality?

DO IT!

- Add your own annotations to the poem, exploring more of its details and their effects. Include the underlined words or phrases.
- Online you will find a copy of the poem with more detailed annotations.

AQA exam-style question

Compare how poets present a sense of threat in 'My Last Duchess' and in one other poem from Power and conflict.

[30 marks]

The Charge of the Light Brigade

Alfred Lord Tennyson (1809 –1892)

1

Half a league, half a league,
Half a league onward,
All in the valley of Death
    Rode the six hundred.
5 'Forward, the Light Brigade!
Charge for the guns!' he said:
Into the valley of Death
    Rode the six hundred.

2

'Forward, the Light Brigade!'
10 Was there a man dismay'd?
Not tho' the soldier knew
    Some one had blunder'd:
Theirs not to make reply,
Theirs not to reason why,
15 Theirs but to do and die:
Into the valley of Death
    Rode the six hundred.

3

Cannon to right of them,
Cannon to left of them,
20 Cannon in front of them
    Volley'd and thunder'd;
Storm'd at with shot and shell,
Boldly they rode and well,
Into the jaws of Death,
25 Into the mouth of Hell
    Rode the six hundred.

4

Flash'd all their sabres bare,
Flash'd as they turn'd in air
Sabring the gunners there,
30   Charging an army, while
     <u>All the world wonder'd</u>:
Plunged in the battery-smoke
Right thro' the line they broke;
Cossack and Russian
35   Reel'd from the sabre-stroke
     Shatter'd and sunder'd.
Then they rode back, but <u>not</u>
     Not the six hundred.

5

Cannon to right of them,
40   Cannon to left of them,
Cannon behind them
     Volley'd and thunder'd;
Storm'd at with <u>sh</u>ot and <u>sh</u>ell,
While <u>h</u>orse and <u>h</u>ero fell,
45   They that had fought so well
Came thro' the jaws of Death
Back from the mouth of Hell,
<u>All that was left of them</u>,
     Left of six hundred.

6

50   <u>When can their glory fade?</u>
O the wild charge they made!
     All the world wonder'd.
<u>Honour the charge they made!</u>
Honour the Light Brigade,
55   <u>Noble</u> six hundred!

Summary

Tennyson imagines the Light Brigade commander urging his cavalry on through a mile-and-a-half-long valley towards the enemy guns. (Notice the heroic, galloping rhythm Tennyson uses for his poem to create a sense of excitement.)

Tennyson reports that the men are not 'dismayed' (disheartened) by knowing that the order to charge is a mistake. They accept that they must not question orders, but take action even if they are likely to die. (Again Tennyson refers to the valley as the 'valley of Death', emphasising that the cavalrymen are unlikely to survive.)

The guns fire at the charging cavalry from three sides – left, right and in front – but the cavalry bravely keep their nerve. (The 600 men ride into the 'jaws of Death'. This **personification** makes the enemy sound like a huge and ferocious monster.)

The cavalry reach the Russian gunners and send them into panic as they slash at them with their swords. Then the cavalry turn and ride back towards their own lines. (Tennyson's **verb** choices suggest the violence and fearlessness of the cavalrymen: 'flash'd', 'plunged', 'shatter'd', 'sunder'd'.)

Tennyson recounts their return journey, again braving the guns on all sides. Many of the cavalry do not return. (Notice Tennyson's ambiguous way of referring to the survivors – 'all that was left of them', perhaps implying horrible deaths and injuries.)

Finally, Tennyson asks us to 'honour' the bravery and sacrifice of the cavalrymen. (Notice how in this very public poem the reader is *told* how to react.)

DEFINE IT!

battery – artillery; heavy guns

Cossack – an ethnic group living in Southern Russia

league – about three miles

Light Brigade – fast, lightly armed cavalry

reel'd – shocked and unable to react

sabre – a sword carried by the cavalry

sunder'd – split apart

Context

In 1854 the Light Brigade was wrongly ordered to attack a Russian artillery position. The heroic charge led to the deaths of nearly 300 men. Tennyson was Britain's national poet (the Poet Laureate) and he wrote his poem shortly after the charge as a public recognition and celebration of the men's heroic act of duty to their country. He also pointed out that a blunder had wasted the men's lives.

See how one student comments on the significance of the public nature of the poem:

> Tennyson's poem has a public purpose: to express and strengthen patriotic feelings. Because of that, the poem is not very subtle: it gallops along in an exciting, heroic way, hardly mentioning the pointless waste of life, and in effect glorifying war.

In the rest of their answer, the student justifies this strong, clear point of view.

DO IT!

Find and list the details the student might use to show their understanding of using context to develop their answer.

Themes

Heroism

The confident rhythm of the poem emphasises how these cavalrymen act without fear or hesitation. The cavalry charge is full of an attractive energy and daring. The horsemen are also highly competent: they 'fought so well', they rode 'well' and are 'noble'.

Compare with
'Kamikaze': contrast the patriotism surrounding the Light Brigade with the failed kamikaze pilot who is condemned and rejected.

Duty

They put duty to their country above their own lives, and readers get the sense that they happily make this sacrifice. The men know that 'some one had blunder'd' but they do not challenge the incompetent order: they obey it without question. They make obedience into an honour.

Compare with
'Bayonet Charge': the charging soldiers have quite different feelings about their duties ('luxuries').

War

The violence of war is hinted at in the violent metaphors for the gunfire that 'volley'd and thunder'd' and 'storm'd at' them. In referring to 'all that was' rather than 'all who were' 'left of them', Tennyson implies not just that many were killed, but that they were torn apart by the gunfire.

Compare with
'Exposure': the soldiers' lives are not glorious at all.

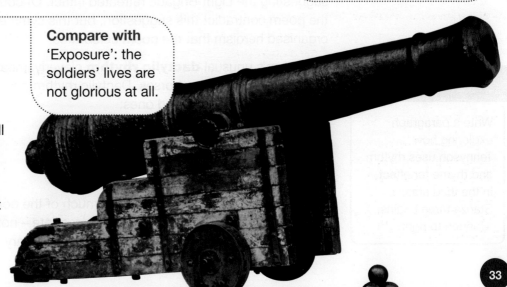

Language

Tennyson clearly wants the poem to appeal to the reader's senses more than their intellect. Therefore he chooses words that help the reader to see, hear and feel the battle: for example, the gunfire is described with a 'thunder' and 'storm' metaphor. The cavalrymen attack the Russians with their 'sabre-stroke', the sibilance imitating the sound of the swords slicing the air. Even Tennyson's word for the error that caused the charge – 'blunder'd' – has a blunt, physical feel. However, he took this word from a newspaper report of the battle and modern readers could respond in varying ways: 'blunder'd' could make us see the commanders as either incompetent, or uncaring; we might view 'blunder'd' as an inappropriately jokey choice.

Tennyson calls the valley the 'valley of Death', not just to remind us that many cavalrymen do not survive, but also to make an emotive link to the Bible's 'valley of the shadow of death'. This allusion (indirect reference) implies that God is on the men's side and that they are doing not just their commander's will, but God's will as well.

Structure and form

The poem is an account of a cavalry charge in the Crimean War. Narrative sequence gives the poem its structure. The openings of stanzas three and five are identical, thus giving symmetry to the charge and the retreat, even suggesting the Light Brigade retreated intact. Of course other details in the poem contradict this suggestion, but this symmetry does convey the organised heroism that the poem celebrates.

The poem's unusual **dactylic rhythm** cleverly imitates the sound and motion of the galloping horses. Dactylic rhythm comprises a stressed syllable followed by two unstressed ones:

> "
>
> <u>Half</u> a league, <u>half</u> a league…
>
> "

This dactylic rhythm gallops through much of the poem, although it falters in those places where it might be less appropriate – notably in the last stanza when the poem shifts from narrative to commentary.

STRETCH IT!

Write a paragraph exploring how Tennyson uses rhythm and rhyme for effect in the third stanza. Stanza three begins, 'Cannon to right…'

The poem's relentless, heroic rhythm is supported by two other important structural features: rhyme and repetition. The poem's rhyming is irregular: for example the first three lines of stanza four are a triplet. In the final, short stanza, lines one, two and four rhyme. Other places in the poem use near, rather than exact, rhymes ('Brigade'/'said'; 'sunder'd'/'hundred'). In 'The Charge of the Light Brigade', rhyme is best seen as part of the repetition of sounds supporting the poem's pace and momentum.

Tennyson repeats lines, words and even sounds – such as the alliterations of '<u>sh</u>ot and <u>sh</u>ell', and '<u>d</u>o and <u>d</u>ie'. All the repetition makes the poem bounce along as though it is a song that would be easy to remember, and perhaps sing along to. Its narrative and its central message of heroic self-sacrifice are easily absorbed: the reader is almost infected by the poem.

DO IT!

Use four different colours to highlight in the poem every:

- alliteration
- rhyme
- repeated word
- repeated line or phrase.

REVIEW IT!

1 How far is half a league?

2 According to Tennyson, how many riders took part in the charge of the Light Brigade?

3 How do we know that Tennyson believed that the British were to blame for the death of so many of the Light Brigade?

4 List three words or phrases that show that the Russians were shocked by the arrival of the Light Brigade.

5 In the third stanza, which metaphor does Tennyson use to describe the Russian gunfire and why?

6 What weapon do the cavalrymen use?

7 What is an allusion? Give an example from the poem.

8 How many of the Light Brigade were killed?

9 How does the poem create a sense of speed and excitement?

10 What is the overall message of the poem?

DO IT!

- Add your own annotations to the poem, exploring more of its details and their effects. Include the underlined words or phrases.
- Online you will find a copy of the poem with more detailed annotations.

AQA exam-style question

Compare how poets present war in 'The Charge of the Light Brigade' and in one other poem from Power and conflict.

[30 marks]

Exposure
Wilfred Owen (1893–1918)

Our brains ache, in the merciless iced east winds that knive us …
Wearied we keep awake because the night is silent …
Low, drooping flares confuse our memory of the salient …
Worried by silence, sentries whisper, curious, nervous,
5   But nothing happens.

Watching, we hear the mad gusts tugging on the wire,
Like twitching agonies of men among its brambles.
Northward, incessantly, the flickering gunnery rumbles,
Far off, like a dull rumour of some other war.
10   What are we doing here?

The poignant misery of dawn begins to grow …
We only know war lasts, rain soaks, and clouds sag stormy.
Dawn massing in the east her melancholy army
Attacks once more in ranks on shivering ranks of grey,
15   But nothing happens.

Sudden successive flights of bullets streak the silence.
Less deadly than the air that shudders black with snow,
With sidelong flowing flakes that flock, pause, and renew,
We watch them wandering up and down the wind's nonchalance,
20   But nothing happens.

Pale flakes with fingering stealth come feeling for our faces –
We cringe in holes, back on forgotten dreams, and stare, snow-dazed,
Deep into grassier ditches. So we drowse, sun-dozed,
Littered with blossoms trickling where the blackbird fusses.
25   – Is it that we are dying?

Slowly <u>our</u> ghosts drag home: glimpsing the sunk fires, glozed
With crusted dark-red jewels; crickets jingle there;
For hours the innocent mice rejoice: the house is theirs;
Shutters and doors, all closed: on us the doors are closed, –
30   We turn back to our dying.

Since <u>we</u> believe not otherwise can kind fires burn;
Nor ever suns smile true on child, or field, or fruit.
For God's invincible spring our love is made afraid;
Therefore, not loath, we lie out here; therefore were born,
35   For love of God seems dying.

Tonight, this frost will fasten on this mud and us,
Shrivelling many hands, puckering foreheads crisp.
The burying-party, picks and shovels in shaking grasp,
Pause over half-known faces. <u>All their eyes are ice</u>,
40   But nothing happens.

DEFINE IT!

brambles – a thorny bush, for example, blackberry

flares – used in war as a signal

flock – to crowd together

glozed – glazed

gunnery – firing of heavy guns

incessantly – constantly

knive – cutting through like a knife

loath – unwilling

melancholy – a sense of sadness

nonchalance – uncaring

poignant – keen sense of sadness

salient – two different meanings: 1 a short trench jutting out towards the enemy line; 2 most important

sentries – a soldier who keeps guard

wire – barbed wire

Summary

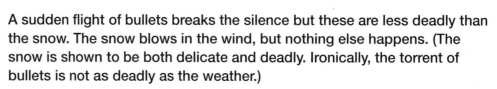

We enter the poem in the middle of the action, with weary and confused soldiers exposed to harsh weather. (These assaults portray weather as an enemy attack.) Men are nervous of the 'silence' but nothing happens. The soldiers are alert and 'watching', at war with the weather as much as the enemy. (The reality of war is shown here as uncomfortable, boring and terrifying.) Distant guns rumble in the north. (The questions within the poem remain unanswered, showing the detachment and hopelessness of the men and their situation.)

Dawn breaks, with misery and greyness. Rain continues and men shiver in cold and wet conditions. (The men are not portrayed as mighty warriors – they shiver as they are exposed to the weather.) Again, nothing happens.

A sudden flight of bullets breaks the silence but these are less deadly than the snow. The snow blows in the wind, but nothing else happens. (The snow is shown to be both delicate and deadly. Ironically, the torrent of bullets is not as deadly as the weather.)

Weather creeps up and the men think about hopes they had for the future before the war. (The men are dehumanised by the conditions and are described as scared animals in holes.) Confused, conditions mean they don't know whether they are dying. (One belief about death is that a person's past life will flash before them. Perhaps the soldiers think this is happening to them.)

The men think of fires, home and sounds of crickets. (The warm images are used as a contrast with the cold conditions.) The narrator reflects that 'doors are closed' to their previous lives. They imagine their homes without them. Their homes are empty and shut up, and taken over by crickets and mice. (Perhaps people at home are losing interest.) With this thought, the men 'turn back' to their dying. (The tone here is blunt and uncaring. Like the people at home, the men are losing interest in whether they live or die.)

Soldiers consider that their suffering has some purpose to keep those at home safe, with 'kind fires'. They think they were 'born' to 'lie out here' and die for their country. They have lost their faith in God. (In his poetry, Owen often speculated on loss of faith in wartime.)

The men fear they will be trapped in the mud and the cold. People arrive to collect the dead, the 'burying party' pausing to look at those they once knew. Still nothing happens.

Context

Wilfred Owen fought and died during World War I, witnessing at first hand the horrors faced by those fighting. He wished to reveal the realities of war – the brutal conditions the soldiers encountered – to a general public fed propaganda about the glory of war.

Themes

Reality of war

The men make the ultimate sacrifice for their country; the poem explores the reality of this sacrifice. This is a war where the men wait as 'nothing happens' and bullets do not kill as many as the weather.

> **Compare with**
> 'The Charge of the Light Brigade': there is a patriotic view of the nobility of war.

Power of nature

Instead of military action and fighting, we are shown soldiers who are battling, unsuccessfully, against the weather. Cold, not bullets, will kill them.

> **Compare with**
> Extract from, 'The Prelude': the narrator is terrified of the 'power' of the peak that looms over him.

Loss and absence

War strips the men of their humanity, their faith and their lives. There is a keen sense of the loss of home and the hopes they had for the future before the war.

> **Compare with**
> 'Bayonet Charge': patriotism, honour and dignity are lost in the face of the terrors of war.

Look at what one student wrote about loss:

In the final stanza, loss of humanity is explored through the detachment shown by the 'burying party' as they arrive to collect the dead. Carrying 'picks and shovels', some remaining shreds of humanity can be seen in the understated emotion as they 'pause' over 'half-known' faces with 'shaking grasp'. However, 'their eyes are ice', revealing this to be a scene that they have lived through many times during this war. Their chilling detachment, like the cold the soldiers face, reminds us that Owen's mission was to ensure the general public understood the horrors of war. The final line, repeating 'But nothing happens', brings the poem full circle as we realise that this devastating loss of life will not change anything.

Using four different colours highlight:

- the focus on the question at the start
- analysis of language in response to the theme
- contextual details to support the theme
- structural details to support the theme.

STRETCH IT!

Write a paragraph to continue this response with your chosen second poem.

Language

The narrator is one of the soldiers facing the horrors of war, and he speaks to the men using inclusive language from the start of the poem: 'Our brains ache', 'We watch them'. It is only with the entrance of the 'burying party' that we get a stranger's view of the scene, bringing some sense of distance and, in this case, detachment.

Owen frequently links weather **imagery** to war: here is a sense of grim irony that it will be the weather and the cold that kills the men rather than bullets and fighting. Nature is personified as a brutal enemy, dressed in grey like the Germans, as the 'winds…knive us…' and the sibilance heard in 'merciless iced east winds' reveals the deathly biting cold that stabs like a knife. Dawn, usually seen as a time of hope and rebirth, brings further 'poignant misery'. This war is not glorious. Instead, the simile of wind tugging at the wire 'like twitching agonies' of men on 'brambles' reveals the struggles and agonies of war. Both the metaphorical 'brambles' (part of the natural world) and the man-made 'wire' have the same devastating effect on the men, perhaps showing how nature has become infected by mankind. Snow moves with 'stealth' as it will 'flock, pause and renew'. This is military language used in battle strategy. The snow's arrival will cause many deaths within these 'shivering ranks'. The repeated 'fl' sounds in 'flowing flakes that flock' shows snow's delicate but deadly nature.

In 'Exposure', Owen creates a sense of monotony and misery: this is not an exciting battle. Instead, the repeated use of ellipsis, 'the night is silent…', indicates how time is dragging as the men wait ('But nothing happens'). The monotony can be clearly seen in the long vowel sounds that drag the pace of the line and signify depression: 'We only know war lasts, rain soaks, and clouds sag stormy'. The repeated 's' sounds in this line couples this monotony with the sound of the rain. Sibilance is used again with the 'Sudden successive flights of bullets', this time imitating the hissing sound of bullets. However, this action is short-lived as monotony returns and 'nothing happens'.

DO IT!

What are the **connotations** of being 'exposed'? Apply two of these connotations to the poem.

Structure and form

The poem is written as eight, five-line stanzas. The fifth line of each stanza acts as a chorus or refrain. This line, repeating 'But nothing happens', speculating on 'dying', or posing an unanswered question, 'What are we doing here?' adds to the sense of paralysis as time stands still with nothing achieved. This, coupled with the use of half-rhyme 'salient/silent' and 'knive us/nervous', adds to the sense of unease. The circular structure of the poem emphasises the futility of war and the futility of their deaths because nothing changes as a result of their sacrifice.

The structure of ideas within the poem reflects the men's thoughts as they wait for something to happen in the grim conditions:

Stanza(s)	Structure of ideas
1–4	Focus on the present, and harsh conditions
5–6	Focus shifts to the past and memories of home
7	Speculates on what war means to you if you lose your faith
8	Speculates on the immediate future; suggests this future will only hold death

REVIEW IT!

1 How is the east wind personified in the first line of the poem?

2 What does 'knive us' suggest about the wind?

3 How does Owen personify dawn?

4 How does Owen describe the snow?

5 How does Owen suggest the soldiers all feel the same way?

6 Write down another example of nature being personified as hostile.

7 What does 'glozed' mean?

8 What might Owen mean by 'For love of God seems dying'?

9 How does 'Exposure' contradict the glorious images of war that were written about in the press during World War I?

10 How might Owen's personal experiences of the war have affected this poem?

DO IT!

- Add your own annotations to the poem, exploring more of its details and their effects. Include the highlighted words or phrases.

- Online you will find a copy of the poem with more detailed annotations.

AQA exam-style question

Compare how poets present a sense of discomfort in 'Exposure' and in one other poem from Power and conflict.

[30 marks]

Storm on the Island
Seamus Heaney (1939–2013)

We are prepared: we build our houses squat,
Sink walls in rock and roof them with good slate.
This wizened earth has never troubled us
With hay, so, as you see, there are no stacks
5   Or stooks that can be lost. Nor are there trees
Which might prove company when it blows full
Blast: you know what I mean – leaves and branches
Can raise a tragic chorus in a gale
So that you can listen to the thing you fear
10   Forgetting that it pummels your house too.
But there are no trees, no natural shelter.
You might think that the sea is company,
Exploding comfortably down on the cliffs
But no: when it begins, the flung spray hits
15   The very windows, spits like a tame cat
Turned savage. We just sit tight while wind dives
And strafes invisibly. Space is a salvo.
We are bombarded by the empty air.
Strange, it is a huge nothing that we fear.

Summary

The narrator explains how they – the islanders – are always prepared for storms, and they are prepared to 'sit them out'. Their houses are designed and built to withstand storms. The island soil is too thin and poor to grow hay, so there are no haystacks to blow away. (The word 'wizened' is usually applied to a person, for example, a 'wizened old man'; 'wizened' and 'troubled' personify the island and its soil.)

He regrets that there are no trees on the island as wind blowing through trees can create a moaning noise, turning the wind into music – 'tragic' music – that makes you forget the destruction it causes. (Heaney's sudden phrase, 'you know what I mean', is strikingly personal and chatty, as though he is appealing to us for the company that trees would give – if there were any.)

DEFINE IT!

gale – very strong wind

hay – grass (or other crops) cut and dried for animal food

salvo – the firing of many guns at once

stooks – a bundle of crop stems, such as grass or wheat

strafes – to attack ground targets from an aircraft

wizened – shrivelled up

Not even the sea is comforting. When the storm comes, the normally 'tame' sea turns 'savage'. While the wind attacks their houses the islanders 'sit tight', waiting for the storm to end. The narrator ends by pointing out the irony that what they fear is literally 'nothing' – just 'empty air'. (However, although he points out that the storm is 'a huge nothing', the poem's end is dense with images of military bombardment to emphasise the storm's power, and the islanders' vulnerability.)

Context

Poets have often presented nature as something comforting and healing for humans, and something that humans are in danger of damaging. However, storms – which are part of nature – are often shown as vicious and spiteful, almost as though they are deliberately attacking humans – perhaps in revenge.

Themes

War

'Storm on the Island' is not literally about war, but the power of the storm is represented by military imagery such as 'blast', 'bombarded'. The islanders are under attack.

> **Compare with** 'Bayonet Charge': here warfare is a matter of fear and panic under fire.

Violence

Although storms might be seen as chaotic, here Heaney shows their violence as calculated and organised. The extended military metaphor strongly conveys this sense of organised violence. However, there is passion in the wind's violence too: it is 'savage'.

> **Compare with** 'Remains': the violence is callous and casual; the target is destroyed.

Nature

Nature leaves the islanders isolated and exposed. They look to it for comfort and shelter, but it offers them none. In the form of storms, nature is hostile and threatens the islanders' existence.

> **Compare with** 'Exposure': similarly, nature is a hostile, threatening force.

Language

Heaney chooses short, hard words to convey the sense of the island as a tough, physical environment, such as 'squat', 'stacks', 'stooks'. The hard alliteration of these last two words further emphasises the harsh island life.

When the storm finally arrives, its spiteful power is expressed through Heaney's extended military metaphor: the wind 'dives' and 'strafes' during the storm's 'bombardment'. Even when the islanders seek comfort in the sea, it is 'Exploding comfortably'. This oxymoron neatly captures nature's potential as both comforter and enemy of people.

Amid all the fear and threat, Heaney keeps using personal appeals to 'you' and 'we', suggesting that people can only survive their conflict with nature by sticking together.

Appropriately the poem is 'noisy', using sound effects to suggest the storm. For example, the sibilance and the alliterative 't' sounds in 'spray hits/…spits like a tame cat' stress the spiteful hissing of the wind.

DO IT!

Find and write down three words or phrases in the poem that show each of the following:

- nature's role as a comforter
- nature's violence.

STRETCH IT!

In what ways does Heaney suggest nature can – in some circumstances – be comforting to humans?

Structure and form

The first six lines are iambic pentameters, giving a measured, confident opening to the poem that justifies the opening claim that 'we are prepared'. From that point on, the poem's even **metre** stumbles and breaks down, supporting the narrator's growing sense of doubt.

The shape of the poem could be seen as dense and rock-like, just like the island itself, and just like the permanent defences the islanders put up against the storms.

The poem is neatly structured according to a chronology that helps the reader to follow its purpose.

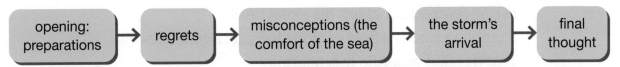

opening: preparations → regrets → misconceptions (the comfort of the sea) → the storm's arrival → final thought

The opening creates a clear focus for readers: the islanders will survive because they have prepared. The ending gives another reason for their survival: the frightening gale is actually 'nothing'.

REVIEW IT!

1 Why do the islanders build their houses 'squat'?

2 Why are there no 'stacks/Or stooks'?

3 Why does Heaney regret that there are no trees on the island?

4 What metaphor does Heaney use to describe the sea spray?

5 What might Heaney mean by 'exploding comfortably'?

6 What **extended metaphor** does Heaney use to describe the storm?

7 What regular metre (rhythm) does Heaney use in part of the poem?

8 Choose one example of alliteration in the poem and explain its effect.

9 Why does Heaney use the word 'strange' in the last line?

10 Why might Heaney have chosen 'Storm on the Island' as the title rather than 'Storm on *an* Island'?

DO IT!

- Add your own annotations to the poem, exploring more of its details and their effects. Include the underlined words or phrases.

- Online you will find a copy of the poem with more detailed annotations.

AQA exam-style question

Compare how poets present violence in 'Storm on the Island' and in one other poem from Power and conflict.

[30 marks]

Bayonet Charge
Ted Hughes (1930–1998)

Suddenly he awoke and was running – raw
In raw-seamed hot khaki, his sweat heavy,
Stumbling across a field of clods towards a green hedge
That dazzled with rifle fire, hearing
5   Bullets smacking the belly out of the air –
He lugged a rifle numb as a smashed arm;
The patriotic tear that had brimmed in his eye
Sweating like molten iron from the centre of his chest, –

In bewilderment then he almost stopped –
10   In what cold clockwork of the stars and the nations
Was he the hand pointing that second? He was running
Like a man who has jumped up in the dark and runs
Listening between his footfalls for the reason
Of his still running, and his foot hung like
15   Statuary in mid-stride. Then the shot-slashed furrows

Threw up a yellow hare that rolled like a flame
And crawled in a threshing circle, its mouth wide
Open silent, its eyes standing out.
He plunged past with his bayonet toward the green hedge,
20   King, honour, human dignity, etcetera
Dropped like luxuries in a yelling alarm
To get out of that blue crackling air
His terror's touchy dynamite.

Summary

The poem explores a moment in time as a soldier runs towards the enemy.

We are dropped straight into the action as the soldier wakes and runs. (Notice that we are not told why he was asleep.) He is sweating and dressed in uniform. He stumbles across the ground amid bullets, awkwardly carrying his rifle. The 'patriotic tear' – his motivation for being a soldier – is lost in the agony of running and the bullets.

Confused, he almost stops running to question what he is doing. He wonders whether he is just a small, insignificant part of the war machine. (His terror is described as someone running in the dark, blindly.) The scene appears in freeze-frame, 'his foot hung' as he questions why he is doing this.

A hare is 'thrown up' out of the furrows in the ploughed ground. It is dying, having been caught up in the battle. He runs past with his bayonet towards a 'green' hedge and the enemy. (The hare is a complex image perhaps representing the destruction of innocence and nature by war.) All the reasons that he had for joining the war are lost as he becomes a weapon in his terror. (The poem ends in the middle of the action, just as it starts in the middle of the action. We do not know if he lives or dies.)

DEFINE IT!

bayonet – a knife attached to the end of a rifle to stab enemy troops

clods – lumps of earth

furrows – a narrow trench made by a plough for planting seeds

lugged – carried with effort

khaki – dull brownish-yellow colour of military uniforms

plunged – hurried without thought

statuary – a group of statues

threshing – moving limbs wildly (a metaphoric meaning)

STRETCH IT!

If the hare is not a real hare, what could it represent? Write a paragraph to explain your ideas.

DO IT!

Look carefully at the description of the hare at the start of the third stanza. How does Hughes want us to feel about the hare? Disgust? Pity? Something else?

Context

Ted Hughes often used images from nature in his poetry to explore a theme or an idea. Probably this poem is set in World War I but we are not told this explicitly (although Hughes reportedly said that this poem was based on imagining the experiences of his father and uncles in the First World War). When soldiers use bayonets on the battlefield, it means they are fighting hand to hand with their enemy.

Themes

The reality of war

The soldier is driven by terror rather than patriotism. He is 'Stumbling' in the mud and is 'In bewilderment'.

Compare with
'Charge of the Light Brigade': here the charge into battle is seen as glorious.

Humanity

The soldier's fear destroys his humanity and he becomes part of the 'clockwork' of the war machine. He becomes a weapon, 'dynamite' with fear driving out the 'luxuries' of 'human dignity, etcetera'.

Compare with
'War Photographer': here it is shown that the experiences of war destroy the lives of those who take part, even after the war.

The natural world

The natural world is used to reflect the innocence of both nature and humans. The hare, 'thrown up' into this conflict, dies in agonies as do the men. Nature is corrupted by this war – the 'green hedge' 'dazzles' with gunfire and the air's 'belly' (its most vulnerable part) is smacked with bullets.

Compare with
'Exposure': nature is personified as hostile.

DOIT!

Choose one more theme relevant to 'Bayonet Charge' and to Power and conflict.

For that theme, list one more poem that you could compare with 'Bayonet Charge'.

Briefly explain your choice.

Language

Through his language choices, Hughes challenges us to consider the difference between patriotic fervour and the reality of war. The use of brutal images (the rifle is compared to a 'smashed arm'; the 'silent' hare's mouth is 'wide/Open silent'; there are 'shot-slashed furrows') combine with images of a man who is running 'in the dark' filled with 'bewilderment'. The third-person narration distances the reader from the running soldier. No one else is present; the enemy is not seen. The only other entity is the dying hare.

DOIT!

List the sights and sounds of war that Hughes gives us.

Hughes portrays the natural world affected by war through his personification of nature: in 'Bullets smacking the belly of the air', the hard 'ck' consonants in 'smacking' directly convey the sound (**onomatopoeia**) and add to the violence. The 'yellow hare' that the earth 'Threw up' innocently into this turmoil suffers agonies, like the soldier who joined up with 'Patriotic tear'. The dramatic 'Threw up' makes us uncomfortable, with connotations of (links to) vomiting and careless actions – this is mankind's impact on nature.

Look at how this student has engaged with the different meanings of 'raw' to explore Hughes' word choice:

> The reader is thrown straight into the battlefield with 'raw' echoing twice in the first two lines. The soldier is 'running - raw', the connotations making us consider his inexperience, his pain and his fear. His uniform, symbolising his part in the war, is 'raw-seamed' - uncomfortable and hurting his legs.

Structure and form

The poem's structure follows the soldier's movement as he charges across the battlefield. The reader is dropped into this battle with a feeling of confusion about what is happening, much like the soldier. The poem's abrupt, unresolved ending could also reflect the abrupt nature of death.

The pace of the poem is linked to the events taking place. In this example we see hyphens, enjambment and repetition: '– raw/In raw-steamed hot khaki' mimicking his 'Stumbling' movement. Enjambment in the second stanza speeds up the pace (we have four lines with no pauses) before the soldier's movement is slowed down with **caesura** after 'Statuary in mid-stride.' as he considers his purpose there. This erratic pace throughout the poem reflects the chaos and confusion the soldier experiences as well as the chaos of war itself.

 **REVIEW IT!**

1 What is meant by 'cold clockwork of stars and nations'?
2 What does 'lugged' suggest about the rifle?
3 What does Hughes mean by 'patriotic tear'?
4 How does Hughes suggest the uniform is uncomfortable?
5 What is meant by 'molten iron…centre of his chest'?
6 What might Hughes mean by 'crawled in a threshing circle'?
7 What does Hughes mean by the phrase 'still running'?
8 Why does the soldier seem to stop on the battlefield?
9 What do you think Hughes wanted us to understand about war?
10 Why does Hughes compare the soldier's terror to 'dynamite'?

 **DO IT!**

- Add your own annotations to the poem, exploring more of its details and their effects. Include the underlined words or phrases.
- Online you will find a copy of the poem with more detailed annotations.

 AQA exam-style question

Compare how poets present fear in 'Bayonet Charge' and in one other poem from Power and conflict.

[30 marks]

Remains
Simon Armitage (b. 1963)

On another occasion, we get sent out
to tackle looters raiding a bank.
And one of them legs it up the road,
probably armed, possibly not.

5   Well myself and somebody else and somebody else
are all of the same mind,
so all three of us open fire.
Three of a kind all letting fly, and I swear

I see every round as it rips through his life –
10 I see broad daylight on the other side.
So we've hit this looter a dozen times
and he's there on the ground, sort of inside out,

pain itself, the image of agony.
One of my mates goes by
15 and tosses his guts back into his body.
Then he's carted off in the back of a lorry.

End of story, except not really.
His blood-shadow stays on the street, and out on patrol
I walk right over it week after week.
20 Then I'm home on leave. But I blink

and he bursts again through the doors of the bank.
Sleep, and he's probably armed, possibly not.
Dream, and he's torn apart by a dozen rounds.
And the drink and the drugs won't flush him out –

25 he's here in my head when I close my eyes,
dug in behind enemy lines,
not left for dead in some distant, sun-stunned, sand-smothered land
or six-feet-under in desert sand,

but near to the knuckle, here and now,
30 his bloody life in my bloody hands.

Summary

A soldier is telling a story of how one day he and two others saw a looter running from a bank. They didn't know if he was armed or not, but were all 'of the same mind' and opened fire. So many bullets hit the looter that his body was destroyed. One of the other soldiers scooped up the looter's guts. A lorry took the body away.

(The soldier's callousness and indifference are summed up in his description of the shot looter as 'sort of inside out', or perhaps it reveals his shock and confusion. Callousness is certainly suggested by Armitage's image of a soldier 'tossing the looter's guts' 'back into his body'. The soldiers treat the looter as meat rather than a person.)

From then on, on patrol or home on leave, the soldier can't help 'seeing' the looter running from the bank, and being shot to pieces. Not even drink or drugs will rid the soldier of these haunting images. Even when he is in action in another part of the world (or metaphorically 'dug' into his own hostile thoughts), the looter stays in his mind's eye. He feels guilty. (It's not just that the soldier begins to feel guilty about the looter's death: it's also that the dead looter seems to be haunting the soldier accusingly.)

DEFINE IT!

looters – people who take advantage of war damage to steal unguarded property

DO IT!

Explain the line: 'He's here in my head when I close my eyes'.

STRETCH IT!

Explain how the soldier-narrator's attitude changes during the poem.

Context

The soldier is likely to be suffering from post-traumatic stress disorder (PTSD). We now accept that PTSD can be both *caused by* disturbing war experiences and be a *cause of* them as well.

Themes

War and conflict

These soldiers seem to have been dehumanised by conflict: they treat other human beings callously, showing them no dignity at all. However, the experience affects them at a deep level, traumatising them.

Compare with
'Exposure': the soldiers here also suffer psychological trauma that disturbs their dreams and their normal values.

Guilt

At first the soldier shows no qualms about his cruelties. Later he is haunted by his victim and by his sense of guilt.

Compare with
'The Charge of the Light Brigade': the commanders are guilty of a 'blunder'.

Inner conflict

The narrator tries to fight off his new feelings of guilt and torment. However, leave, sleep, alcohol and drugs are not powerful enough to suppress his emerging sense of guilt.

Compare with
'War Photographer': the narrator tries to control his nightmare memories by ordering them into a series of photos.

DOIT!

Find one more theme relevant to 'Remains' and to Power and conflict.

For that theme, list one more poem that you could compare with 'Remains'.

Briefly explain your choice.

Language

At the start of the poem, because the soldier is desensitised to his experiences, his language is full of bravado and has a style of casual indifference that does not match the seriousness of his actions: the soldiers are 'letting fly' with their guns; the victim's body is 'inside out'; one of them 'tosses the guts' of the victim. The whole tone of the vocabulary and style is casual.

In the poem's second half, when the soldier can no longer detach himself from his actions, the language becomes more original and metaphoric: for example, he cannot rid his mind of the victim's 'blood-shadow'; he cannot forget the way he used to be in the 'sun-stunned' land.

See how one student explores the effects of Armitage's language in the final line:

'Bloody' is a swear word that expresses the soldier's desperate desire to turn back the clock, but it is literal too: it graphically reminds us of the ripped-up body and the hands that scooped up its guts.

Structure and form

The poem balances on the phrase, 'except not really'. Up to that point the victim is presented as a target without feelings or worth. After that point, the narrator expresses his mental torment as his conscience takes over, and his trauma and guilt deepen.

The poem is a dramatic monologue, and to make the soldier-narrator's voice authentic, Armitage writes in the way an ordinary soldier might speak, telling the story in the present tense, making it boastfully dramatic at first. The narrative is also full of slang and informal word choices, much more typical of speech than writing.

See how one student supports this point with a neat use of quotations:

> Armitage gives us a sense of a real soldier talking (rather than writing) by the use of **colloquial** word choices: for example, he says the looter 'legs it' rather than 'runs', and 'letting fly' rather than 'firing'. This style sounds just like someone telling a story - it's dramatic and immediate.

REVIEW IT!

1 Where did the soldiers find the looter?

2 How many soldiers were there?

3 How many shots hit the looter?

4 What does the narrator mean by 'inside out'?

5 What is the effect on the reader of 'tosses the guts'?

6 Why is it 'not really' the end of the story?

7 What does the narrator mean by 'the drink and the drugs *won't flush him out*'?

8 What does the narrator mean by 'dug in behind enemy lines'?

9 Why are the narrator's hands 'bloody'?

10 Why do you think the poem is called 'Remains'?

DO IT!

- Add your own annotations to the poem, exploring more of its details and their effects. Include the underlined words or phrases.

- Online you will find a copy of the poem with more detailed annotations.

AQA exam-style question

Compare how poets present guilt in 'Remains' and in one other poem from Power and conflict.

[30 marks]

Poppies
Jane Weir (b. 1963)

Three days before Armistice <u>Sunday</u>
and poppies had already been <u>placed</u>
on individual war graves. Before <u>you</u> left,
I pinned one onto <u>your</u> lapel, crimped petals,
5   spasms of paper red, <u>disrupting a blockade</u>
of yellow bias binding around your blazer.

Sellotape bandaged around my hand,
I rounded up as many white cat hairs
as I could, <u>smoothed down your shirt's</u>
10 <u>upturned collar</u>, steeled the softening
of my face. I wanted to graze my nose
across the tip of your nose, play at
being Eskimos like we did when
you were little. <u>I resisted the impulse</u>
15 to run my fingers through the <u>gelled</u>
<u>blackthorns of your hair</u>. All my words
flattened, rolled, turned into felt,

slowly melting. I was brave, as I walked
with you, to the front door, threw
20 it open, the world overflowing
<u>like a treasure chest</u>. A split second
and you were away, <u>intoxicated</u>.
After you'd gone I went into your bedroom,
<u>released a song bird from its cage</u>.
25 Later a <u>single dove</u> flew from the pear tree,
and this is where it has led me,
skirting the church yard walls, my stomach busy
<u>making tucks, darts, pleats</u>, hat-less, <u>without</u>
<u>a winter coat or reinforcements</u> of scarf, gloves.

30 On reaching the top of the hill I <u>traced</u>
<u>the inscriptions</u> on the war memorial,
leaned against it <u>like a wishbone</u>.
The dove pulled freely against the sky,
an <u>ornamental stitch</u>. I listened, hoping to hear
35 <u>your playground voice catching on the wind</u>.

Summary

We cannot be sure exactly what happens in the poem. Probably Jane Weir was deliberately ambiguous so that the poem could capture the feelings of any mother who has lost their child to school, the army or even death.

One early November the narrator, a mother, pins a poppy to the lapel of her son's blazer. (The blazer suggests this is a school uniform.) She then recalls (probably) another time when she smartens up her son's appearance, suppressing her urge to show her deep love for him. (We don't know where he is going, but his spiky, gelled hair would suggest it is not – at this time – the army.)

She releases him into the exciting outside world and also releases 'a song bird from its cage'. (This is probably a metaphor for the release of her own pent-up emotions: perhaps the 'song' is her tears.)

Unprepared, her stomach churning, she follows a dove (a symbol of peace and hope) to the top of the hill outside, where she traces the names on the war memorial. She listens out for her son's 'playground voice' in the air. (She is probably yearning to gather him back into the safety of childhood. It is even possible that her own son's name is on the war memorial.)

Context

Immediately after World War I, poppies were the only flower that grew on the battlefields. The poppy is the symbol of remembrance for the millions who lost their lives in battle then, and in conflicts up to the present day.

DEFINE IT!

Armistice Sunday – Remembrance Sunday in early November

bias binding – decorative edging for clothes

blackthorn – a spiky bush, or just the thorn of the bush

blockade – a military barrier, for example to stop supplies getting to an enemy

crimped – squeezed together

spasms – uncontrolled movements of the body

tucks (darts, pleats) – folds (in an item of clothing)

wishbone – a chicken bone associated with luck

DO IT!

Briefly explain why the narrator might have compared herself with a wishbone.

STRETCH IT!

Explain what the poem's final line might mean.

Themes

War

Armistice Sunday and its poppy symbols, and the war memorial on the hill give the poem its war context. The poem is for all mothers who have lost loved ones in conflicts.

Compare with
'Exposure': a soldier relates the stresses of front-line warfare but thinks of the home he has left behind.

Inner conflict

The mother narrator is torn between giving her son freedom, respecting his desire for independence, and her desire to limit and protect him.

Compare with
'Remains': the narrator is torn between bravado and a deepening sense of responsibility.

Suffering

Her suffering is restrained and dignified. It expresses itself in her confusion and recklessness as she follows the dove up the hill.

Compare with
'Storm on the Island': the islanders endure and wait in hope.

DO IT!

Choose two more themes relevant to 'Poppies' and to Power and conflict.

For each theme, list one more poem that you could compare with 'Poppies'.

Briefly explain each of your choices.

Language

Although the poem tries to express a universal experience – all mothers and all their sons – it is personal in tone, being addressed to 'you', the narrator's son.

The poem's effect depends on its imagery: its interaction of literal pictures (for example, the poppy being pinned on to a lapel) and powerful images that capture the complicated feelings associated with losing a child. The narrator recognises that for her son 'the world [is]…like a treasure chest.' This simile suggests the world is offering itself to the son, enticing him – as jewels do. As he leaves he is 'intoxicated', a metaphor that neatly sums up his inability to resist the temptations the world seems to promise.

At the heart of the poem's imagery are the clothing metaphors: the pinned red poppy 'disrupts' the restrictive 'yellow…binding' around the boy's blazer. To calm herself, the mother 'smoothed down' her son's collar. Later, when her son has abruptly left, the mother imagines her emotional turmoil as 'tucks, darts and pleats' in her stomach.

Structure and form

'Poppies' is a dramatic monologue spoken not by Weir but by an unnamed mother – a sort of 'everymother'. Without rhyme or consistent rhythm, the poem is quiet and thoughtful, as is appropriate to the mother's strong, but controlled emotions.

The poem's central feature that binds it all together is the recurring bird and clothing imagery. Behind the clothing image is our understanding that clothes are decorative and express a person's personality and values, but clothes also hide and confine. In the first stanza, the dignity and formality of the public grieving on 'Armistice Sunday' is reinforced by the boy's uniform. However, the uniform is 'disrupted' by the poppy's 'spasms of paper red'. We see that clothes are not quite managing to conceal and confine. Towards the end of the poem, Weir has clothing come apart symbolically: the 'tucks, pleats, darts' the mother's stomach makes are a sign of her emotional release and turmoil, and she escapes the house without the 'reinforcements' of suitable clothing.

 **REVIEW IT!**

1 When had poppies been placed on soldiers' graves?

2 What does the narrator pin to her son's blazer?

3 Why does she wrap her hand in 'Sellotape'?

4 What do we learn about the boy's hair from the description, 'gelled/blackthorns'?

5 Why does she resist the temptation to run her fingers through her son's hair?

6 What does she release in her son's bedroom?

7 What does a dove traditionally symbolise?

8 What does she do at the top of the hill?

9 Why does the narrator trace the inscriptions on the war memorial?

10 In what ways is 'Poppies' a 'dramatic monologue'?

 **DO IT!**

- Add your own annotations to the poem, exploring more of its details and their effects. Include the underlined words or phrases.
- Online you will find a copy of the poem with more detailed annotations.

 ### AQA exam-style question

Compare how poets present suffering in 'Poppies' and in one other poem from Power and conflict.

[30 marks]

War Photographer
Carol Ann Duffy (b. 1955)

In his darkroom he is finally alone
with spools of suffering set out in ordered rows.
The only light is red and softly glows,
as though this were a church and he
5   a priest preparing to intone a Mass.
Belfast. Beirut. Phnom Penh. All flesh is grass.

He has a job to do. Solutions slop in trays
beneath his hands, which did not tremble then
though seem to now. Rural England. Home again
10 to ordinary pain which simple weather can dispel,
to fields which don't explode beneath the feet
of running children in a nightmare heat.

Something is happening. A stranger's features
faintly start to twist before his eyes,
15 a half-formed ghost. He remembers the cries
of this man's wife, how he sought approval
without words to do what someone must
and how the blood stained into foreign dust.

A hundred agonies in black-and-white
20 from which his editor will pick out five or six
for Sunday's supplement. The reader's eyeballs prick
with tears between the bath and pre-lunch beers.
From the aeroplane he stares impassively at where
he earns his living and they do not care.

Summary

This poem is about a war photographer who has returned from a war zone to develop his photographs in readiness for publication.

The photographer is in his darkroom with his reels of film. The red safe light is on. He has a task to do and he puts the developing solution into the trays. His hands tremble now but were steady when he was doing his job in the war zone. He is back in 'Rural England', where people don't suffer except to complain about the weather, and children can run across fields without being blown up.

The photographic image begins to appear. He thinks back to the cries of the wife of the man in the image (presumably the man is dead). He needed to ask her permission to take the photograph, but he didn't have the language to do so. (Notice that the ethics of taking photographs of pain and suffering are being questioned here. The photographer covers his guilt by telling himself that 'someone must' do this.)

The photographer has hundreds of painful images. His editor will pick out five or six for the Sunday newspaper's magazine. The reader will be saddened by these images, but will soon move on with their comfortable lives. The photographer knows that ultimately people don't care. (Duffy is suggesting that the pictures and the readers' sadness is just another form of entertainment.)

DEFINE IT!

darkroom – a room for developing photographs where normal light is excluded

dispel – to make a doubt or a feeling disappear

impassively – not showing any emotion

intone – to recite in a way that sounds like chanting

Mass – a religious ceremony

rural England – the countryside of England

solutions – chemicals used to develop photographs

spools – rolls of film

Sunday's supplement – a free glossy magazine in a Sunday newspaper

Context

We often see shocking images on television, the internet and newspapers. A war photographer goes into war zones and battlefields to record these events and images.

Photographic film is sensitive to white light, so a darkroom is designed to keep out any ordinary light. A red safe light is used. Photographic images are developed in chemicals and appear slowly once placed in the chemical solution.

DO IT!

Research the photographs by Don McCullin – a famous war photographer – to help you understand the poem's context.

Themes

The reality of war

The poem explores the contrast between the comfort of 'Rural England', where people consume the photographer's images before 'pre-lunch beers', and the reality of 'the blood stained into foreign dust' for the people caught up in the conflict.

Compare with
'Poppies': the reality of war is seen through the eyes of family members.

Inner conflict

The photographer goes into war zones to report and record images of conflict. However, these 'hundred agonies' are reduced to 'five or six' photographs in a free Sunday magazine. The photographer's guilt is shown by his trembling hands as he justifies his actions as earning 'his living'.

Compare with
'Kamikaze': the pilot is caught between his duty and his wish to live.

Distance and detachment

The poem explores the emotional distance that the photographer feels for the subjects of his photographs. It's how he 'earns his living'. This is shared by the reaction of his readers who are emotional for a moment but then get on with their lives.

Compare with
'London': the narrator wanders through London's streets and notices the exhaustion, illness and unhappiness in the faces around him – almost like he's photographing them.

Language

The poem's language explores the distance between the horrors of war and our growing indifference to these horrors. The poem opens with the photographer imposing order on the 'spools of suffering', a metaphor for the horrors contained in the photographs. The film spools are set out in 'ordered rows' likening them to body bags or graves.

Religious images are used to reveal his inner conflict. The darkroom is 'a church' and the photographer 'intones a Mass', linking the room to confession and worship – celebrating and regretting the actions performed as part of his job. The names of war zones, 'Belfast. Beirut. Phnom Penh.' and the decisive use of full stops emphasise this new holy trinity.

Contrasts between the comfort of 'Rural England' with 'simple weather' and 'fields which don't explode' with the 'nightmare heat' and 'blood stained' dust are used to reveal the difference between people at home and the people in the photographs. Duffy reveals the complacency of people whose 'eyeballs prick/with tears' in the short amount of time between 'the bath' and 'beers' as they look and then move on.

Structure and form

The poem is written in four, six-line regular stanzas. Each stanza finishes with a rhyming couplet, giving a sensation of creating order out of chaos – just like the photographer tries to do within the darkroom. The internal rhyme of 'beers' and 'tears' in stanza four reinforces the indifferent attitude of those who look at the images before returning to their comfortable lives. Lines two and three rhyme as well, with a half rhyme in the final stanza.

The poem's ideas are ordered into a sequence for logic and effect – like the photos. The poem leads us through the process of developing the photographs before giving us a glimpse of the horrors of the conflict in stanzas two and three. Stanza four shifts to the lives of people who will view these images, 'agonies', before the poem comes full circle in the final couplet with the photographer 'impassively' flying out to another assignment on an aeroplane.

REVIEW IT!

1. In what sense are the reels of photographs 'spools of suffering'?
2. What phrase means 'All human life is transitory, temporary'?
3. What might Duffy mean by 'He has a job to do'?
4. How many photographs will the editor pick out?
5. What might Duffy mean by 'A stranger's features/faintly start to twist before his eyes'?
6. Explain why the photographer's hands 'tremble' in the darkroom.
7. What might Duffy mean by 'A hundred agonies in black-and-white'?
8. Give a possible reason why 'The reader's eyeball's prick/with tears'.
9. What might be the impact of the internal rhyme of 'beers' and 'tears' in stanza four?
10. Explain the different types of conflict in the poem.

DO IT!

- Add your own annotations to the poem, exploring more of its details and their effects. Include the underlined words or phrases.
- Online you will find a copy of the poem with more detailed annotations.

AQA exam-style question

Compare how poets present attitudes towards conflict in 'War Photographer' and in one other poem from Power and conflict.

[30 marks]

Tissue

Imtiaz Dharker (b.1954)

Paper that lets the <u>light</u>
<u>shine</u> through, this
is what could alter things.
Paper thinned by age or touching,

5   the kind you find in well-used books,
the back of the Koran, where a hand
has written in the names and histories,
who was born to whom,

the height and weight, who
10   died where and how, on which sepia date,
pages smoothed and stroked and turned
transparent with attention.

If buildings were paper, I might
feel their <u>drift</u>, see how easily
15   they fall away on a sigh, a <u>shift</u>
in the direction of the wind.

Maps too. The <u>sun shines</u> through
their borderlines, the marks
that rivers make, roads,
20   railtracks, mountainfolds,

Fine slips from grocery shops
that say how much was sold
and what was paid by credit card
might fly our lives like paper kites.

25   An architect could use all this,
place layer over layer, <u>luminous</u>
script over numbers over line,
and never wish to build again with brick

or block, but let the <u>daylight</u> break
30 through capitals and monoliths,
through the shapes that pride can make,
find a way to trace a grand design

with living tissue, raise a structure
never meant to last,
35 of paper smoothed and stroked
and thinned to be transparent,

turned into your skin.

Summary

The poem explores what is important in our lives and the power of the records we create on paper as well as the stories paper can tell about our lives.

Stanzas one to three

Paper has the power to 'alter things'. The narrator considers the paper used in religious books and the knowledge these 'well-used books' contain when they have been used to record family births and deaths. Family connections and relationships can change when they are examined closely or develop over time, 'Paper thinned by age or touching'. The power of recording our history and making records of the past helps us to gain knowledge as the truth becomes clear ('transparent') with this 'attention', as we study the past.

Stanzas four to six

Paper may be fragile but it controls our lives in a number of ways. The narrator speculates on what would happen if buildings (representing our society) were made out of paper. They could 'drift' or 'shift', move in the wind. Maps, made of paper, help us to make journeys but also show our 'borderlines', the things that restrict us. However, borders are temporary whereas knowledge, 'the sun' shining through these maps, is permanent. Money is another important aspect of our life. It can control us, 'fly our lives' or

through the 'fine slips', the record of what we have bought we can tell the story of our lives.

Stanzas seven and eight

Paper provides the starting point for our society – the architect's designs on paper for buildings. Yet these mighty designs – 'capitals and monoliths' – that show our society's pride is nothing in comparison to a 'grand design': facing what is important in our lives. Our power will be shown through our 'tissue', not these buildings.

Stanzas nine and ten

Paper is 'tissue' – human skin. The narrator links the architect's design to God's grand design and then to human skin, 'living tissue'. This skin was 'never made to last'. It is temporary and fragile. However, through the creation of human life, 'turned into your skin', we will outlast buildings and paper records of our history. (The abrupt shift to the personal 'your' is interesting here. Is it the reader?)

DEFINE IT!

fine slips – shopping receipts

Koran – central religious text of Islam

luminous – giving off light; shining

monoliths – large and characterless buildings; large blocks of stone often used as pillars

sepia – a reddish-brown colour usually seen in old photographs

transparent – a material that can be seen through

Context

Imtiaz Dharker, a poet and film-maker, was born in Pakistan but grew up in Scotland. Her poetry often looks at themes of identity, gender and politics. She was inspired to write the poem after finding her name and date of birth written by her father on the pages of a book. This led her to consider what is important in life and the connections we make and lose.

Themes

Power and fragility

Paper is both powerful because it records history and we can learn from it, yet fragile because it is easily destroyed. It is 'thinned by age or touching' – like human life. 'Tissue' is also used in idioms within our culture, for example, 'tissue thin' meaning very fine, almost transparent and 'tissue of lies' meaning a number of lies or false statements made to hide the truth deliberately. 'Tissue paper' is also used to wrap or protect delicate objects.

> **Compare with**
> 'Ozymandias': power is temporary however mighty the ruler.

Identity

The poem explores how human life, although temporary, will continue through 'living tissue' – our 'skin'. Our skin, our identity, is more important than the buildings we create to make ourselves seem powerful. We can also trace and record our family history through accessing papers and family records.

> **Compare with**
> 'Checking Out Me History': focuses on the conflict and struggle within personal identity.

Power of knowledge

If we let knowledge, 'the light/shine through' we can 'alter things'.

> **Compare with**
> 'London': here, 'mind-forged manacles' which hide the truth.

DO IT!

Look carefully at this response from a student exploring the theme of family history in the poem. Find and highlight the following examples:

- introducing the theme
- using quotations to reinforce their ideas
- explaining the impact of this theme on the reader.

The poem explores the power of family history within a life that 'was never meant to last'. Dharker shows us that, even within our temporary lives, our power comes from the connections we make in our lives, through the 'names and histories' written into 'well-used books'. The reader understands Dharker's message, that these histories, even coming from everyday 'fine slips', are more powerful than any 'capitals or monoliths' that we build. Instead, it is our skin, our 'living tissue', that is both fragile and powerful.

Language

Paper is used as an extended metaphor for the power of humankind as well as the fragility of that power. The poem explores where paper is used within our lives, from the humble 'fine slips' of shopping receipts, to the romance of 'Maps' with their 'railtracks, mountainfolds', and the sacred pages of religious books, 'the Koran' with its 'well-used' pages. Yet these examples are fragile: 'Paper is thinned by age or touching', it can 'easily…fall away on a sigh' or might 'fly our lives' just like 'paper kites'.

Images of light are used throughout the poem to explore knowledge in terms of learning about life or through religious truth. Through this positive force in our lives, 'light' enables us to 'alter', or change things, in our lives. Through its power, we can understand the restrictions, or 'borderlines' on the 'Maps' of our lives. 'The sun shines through' these restrictions, making them temporary. The sun, representing truth and light, is permanent. Even the symbols of civilisation and political power, 'the capitals and monoliths', have no power in the face of 'daylight' that breaks through these constructions. Light, either meaning knowledge or religious truth, is seen as an all-powerful force in human existence.

The title of the poem has many connotations: from the link with paper to human tissue – skin. However, there are also connotations of human emotions and mopping up tears, as well as the knowledge gained from old books, or religious texts.

Look at the statements listed below. Find a quotation to reinforce each statement.

1 Dharker uses paper as a symbol of what is important in life.

2 Dharker sees paper as an image of power that can be written on to record the power of a whole people.

3 Dharker sees paper, like power, as fragile and temporary and susceptible to human touch, to their imprint.

4 Dharker sees skin that enfolds each of us as another form of paper.

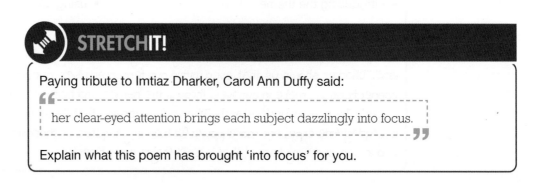

STRETCHIT!

Paying tribute to Imtiaz Dharker, Carol Ann Duffy said:

" her clear-eyed attention brings each subject dazzlingly into focus. "

Explain what this poem has brought 'into focus' for you.

Structure and form

The poem is written in irregular four-lined stanzas until the final stanza, which stands alone with only one line, reflecting the sudden and surprising change of emphasis from paper to skin. The use of enjambment allows the lines to flow, like paper that falls away 'on a sigh'. The use of internal rhyme, such as 'drift' and 'shift', allows the words to mimic this movement of paper in the wind, while the structure of ideas presents a seamless transition between paper, light, history and life.

Stanza(s)	Structure of ideas
1–3	Focus on recording our history on paper.
4–6	Explore the fragility of paper despite the control it has over our lives.
7–10	Explore the conflict between humans and their environment, reflecting on how they could exist in harmony.

 **REVIEW IT!**

1 In the first stanza, how do we know that the paper is thin?

2 What does 'sepia' mean?

3 What everyday uses are we are shown for paper?

4 What are 'fine slips'?

5 What do we learn about books in the phrase 'well-used' books?

6 Who does the narrator suggest could use all the paper in the world?

7 Why might that person prefer paper to bricks?

8 Who do you think is the 'you' in the phrase 'your skin'?

9 How does the poet suggest that money controls us?

10 Why has the poet called the poem 'Tissue' and not 'Paper'?

 **DO IT!**

- Add your own annotations to the poem, exploring more of its details and their effects. Include the underlined words or phrases.
- Online you will find a copy of the poem with more detailed annotations.

 AQA exam-style question

Compare how poets present the fragile nature of power in 'Tissue' and in one other poem from Power and conflict.

[30 marks]

The Emigrée
Carol Rumens (b.1944)

There once was a country... I left it as a child
but my memory of it is sunlight-clear
for it seems I never saw it in that November
which, I am told, comes to the mildest city.
5   The worst news I receive of it cannot break
my original view, the bright, filled paperweight.
It may be at war, it may be sick with tyrants,
but I am branded by an impression of sunlight.

The white streets of that city, the graceful slopes
10 glow even clearer as time rolls its tanks
and the frontiers rise between us, close like waves.
That child's vocabulary I carried here
like a hollow doll, opens and spills a grammar.
Soon I shall have every coloured molecule of it.
15 It may by now be a lie, banned by the state
but I can't get it off my tongue. It tastes of sunlight.

I have no passport, there's no way back at all
but my city comes to me in its own white plane.
It lies down in front of me, docile as paper;
20 I comb its hair and love its shining eyes.
My city takes me dancing through the city
of walls. They accuse me of absence, they circle me.
They accuse me of being dark in their free city.
My city hides behind me. They mutter death,
25 and my shadow falls as evidence of sunlight.

Summary

The poem is told from the point of view of a person looking back at the city of their childhood.

The narrator thinks back to the city she left as a child. (We are not told the name of the city or the country, so perhaps it represents any place of conflict.) Her memories are filled with sunlight. She reflects that even the 'worst news' about her country cannot darken her memories. (Notice the folk-tale-style opening that links to childhood. It is followed by an ellipsis, suggesting a pause or perhaps a shift in time.)

The narrator considers the beauty of the city, but time has moved on relentlessly. (The images of tanks and frontiers to show the march of time dramatically contrast with the heavenly 'white streets' of the city. This use of 'white' gives an idealised view of the city and links to light images.) She reflects on her vocabulary that she remembers from childhood, suggesting that it is now banned by the state but remains on her 'tongue'.

The narrator returns to the present and states that she cannot return to the city. She has her childhood memories of the city, but as an adult she knows that, in reality, the city is full of dark and hostile forces. (The city is personified as a gentle, loving creature linking back to the fairy-tale opening of the poem. The ruling forces are threatening and accusing. Some critics believe that these hostile forces relate to the narrator's feelings of isolation and oppression in her adopted city.) Despite this oppression, the poem ends with hope and sunlight.

DEFINE IT!

branded – a mark made with a hot iron to show ownership

docile – dutiful and obedient

emigrée (also émigré) – a person who has left their country to live in another, usually for political reasons

frontier – a border separating two countries

paperweight – an ornament designed to keep papers in place on a desk

tyrants – cruel rulers

DO IT!

What is the main difference between the city and the narrator's memory of it?

Context

Taken from a collection, *Thinking of Skin*, Carol Rumens's poetry often focuses on issues regarding culture and a sense of place. An emigrée is someone who has relocated to another country, often because of war or political conflict.

Themes

Memory

The poem contains childhood memories of a city that the narrator left as a child. These idealised memories are filled with 'sunlight', positivity and hope.

Compare with
Extract from, 'The Prelude': here childhood memory is filled with contrasting feelings of positivity and fear.

Identity

The narrator's first language, the 'child's vocabulary', gives the narrator their sense of identity. This language has been 'carried' to the new country 'like a hollowed doll'. Even though the new rulers of the country now ban this language, she doesn't lose her language and 'can't get it off my tongue'.

Compare with
'Kamikaze': the pilot's failure to complete his patriotic mission leads to a loss of identity when his community and family shun him, treating him as if 'he no longer existed'.

Time

Time, depicted as rolling 'tanks', enables the adult to understand the reality of the 'dark', hostile forces compared with the sunlit childhood memories.

Compare with
'Poppies': time gradually erases the memory of the woman's son ('inscriptions on the war memorial').

Language

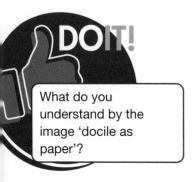

What do you understand by the image 'docile as paper'?

Images of light and darkness run throughout the poem. Childhood memories are 'sunlight-clear' with light used to show positivity and clarity. The narrator acknowledges that these memories cannot be broken by 'the worst news' as they are 'branded' – burned painfully and permanently – on to her mind. This mixture of positive images of light linked with darker images continues throughout the poem. In the third stanza, we see the city personified as a gentle creature, 'docile as paper', that she pets before it 'takes her dancing' like a lover. Once again, we are shown the difference between her childhood idealised memories and the reality of her view as an adult.

STRETCHIT!

Which other poem from the Power and conflict cluster links with the image from 'The Emigrée' described below?

'Hollow doll' is a complex image. It links to the 'child's vocabulary'. This vocabulary – the first language, now 'banned by the state...spills' out. It is a 'doll', a child's toy, but as it is 'hollow' it suggests that it is empty, meaning perhaps that she has been stripped of her language and culture. She can't forget this language: 'Can't get it off my tongue'.

Structure and form

The poem is written as a first person account from the perspective of someone who is reflecting on her original home city. The country and city are not named, perhaps ensuring that this is seen as any area of conflict, any place of oppression.

Written in three fairly consistent stanzas (eight-eight-nine lines), each stanza ends with an image of sunlight, taking the reader back to the narrator's positive childhood memories of the city.

The key ideas in the poem explore the power of memory:

Stanza	Key ideas
1	Childhood memories are presented as 'sunlight-clear' even though the adult knows the reality of 'worst news'.
2	Memories are shown to become 'ever clearer' over time and language, 'tastes of sunlight'.
3	These memories are solidified as the city is protected by her memories even though she understands the hostile forces that now rule it.

 **STRETCHIT!**

The opening of the poem begins like a folk or fairy tale. What further links with fairy tales can you find in the poem?

 **REVIEW IT!**

1 What or who is an 'emigrée'?

2 Where is the country that the narrator left?

3 How are the last lines of the stanza similar to each other?

4 What colour is used to describe the streets of the city?

5 What type of story usually begins with 'There once was…'?

6 Who has banned her language?

7 Find a simile used to describe the city.

8 How do we know that the city is now a hostile place?

9 How are the frontiers described?

10 Explain the difference in the poem between '*my* city' and '*the* city'.

 **DOIT!**

- Add your own annotations to the poem, exploring more of its details and their effects. Include the underlined words or phrases.

- Online you will find a copy of the poem with more detailed annotations.

 ## AQA exam-style question

Compare how poets present the power of place in 'The Emigrée' and in one other poem from Power and conflict.

[30 marks]

Checking Out Me History
John Agard (b. 1949)

Dem tell me
Dem tell me
Wha dem want to tell me

Bandage up me eye with me own history
5   Blind me to me own identity

Dem tell me bout 1066 and all dat
dem tell me bout Dick Whittington and he cat
But Toussaint L'Ouverture
no dem never tell me bout dat

10   *Toussaint*
        a slave
        with vision
        lick back
        Napoleon
15   *battalion*
        and first Black
        Republic born
        Toussaint de thorn
        to de French
20   *Toussaint de beacon*
        of de Haitian Revolution

Dem tell me bout de man who discover de balloon
and de cow who jump over de moon
Dem tell me bout de dish ran away with de spoon
25   but dem never tell me bout Nanny de maroon

Nanny
see-far woman
of mountain dream
fire-woman struggle
30 *hopeful stream*
to freedom river

Dem tell me bout Lord Nelson and Waterloo
but dem never tell me bout Shaka de great Zulu
Dem tell me bout Columbus and 1492
35 but <u>what happen to de Caribs and de Arawaks too</u>

Dem tell me bout Florence Nightingale and <u>she</u> lamp
and how Robin Hood used to camp
Dem tell me bout ole King Cole was a merry ole soul
but dem never tell me bout Mary Seacole

40 *From Jamaica*
she travel far
to the Crimean War
she volunteer to go
and even when de British said no
45 *she still brave the Russian snow*
<u>a healing star</u>
among the wounded
<u>a yellow sunrise</u>
to the dying

50 Dem tell me
Dem tell me wha dem want to tell me
But now I <u>checking out me own history</u>
I <u>carving out</u> me identity

Summary

The narrator complains that history taught in British schools excludes historical figures with special significance for Afro-Caribbeans.

He complains that the exclusion of black historical figures blinds him to his own identity. He suggests that some traditional history – for example, Dick Whittington and the Battle of Hastings – is trivial compared with the role of a Caribbean hero such as Toussaint L'Ouverture, who beat the French and inspired independence for Haiti. He also suggests that schools pay more attention to nursery rhymes than to heroes such as Nanny of the Maroons, whose vision and fight brought freedom to many.

Nanny of the Maroons

Agard continues to point out official history's unequal treatment of white British and black historical figures. He celebrates the bravery and determination of black heroes such as Mary Seacole, a Jamaican nurse in the Crimean War.

He concludes by announcing that he is now finding out about his 'own history' – the history of people that Afro-Caribbeans can be proud of. He sees this process of historical (re-)discovery as 'carving out' his real identity. (The metaphor, 'carving out', emphasises that he is going to force Afro-Caribbean history into the record. It reminds us of carving initials into wood to make an identity permanent and noticeable.)

DEFINE IT!

Caribs and Arawaks – original inhabitants of Caribbean islands

Columbus – the leader of the first Europeans to discover the Caribbean islands

Florence Nightingale – an English nurse who became famous in the Crimean War (1853–56) as 'The Lady with the Lamp', which she carried from bed to bed

Lord Nelson – commander of the victorious British fleet at the Battle of Trafalgar (1805)

Mary Seacole – a British-Jamaican nurse who became famous for the hospital she set up to treat injured soldiers in the Crimean War

Nanny de maroon – a slave rebellion leader in the 1700s, now a national hero in Jamaica

Shaka – a Zulu king at the beginning of the 1800s

Toussaint L'Ouverture – a Caribbean hero who beat the French and inspired independence for Haiti

Waterloo – the 1815 battle in which the British and Germans defeated Napoleon's French army

Context

Two hundred years ago, Toussaint L'Ouverture, a black slave, led a revolution on the French part of a Caribbean island. Haiti finally defeated France and won independence, a victory that inspired slave rebellions throughout the Caribbean, and showed that black slaves did not need to rely on liberal white people for their freedom. John Agard grew up in the Caribbean.

Nowadays we understand that language and history are vital to a people's sense of identity.

Toussaint L'Ouverture

NAILIT!

Context is only relevant if it sheds light on the poems and your exam question. Look at these two students' comments on context. The first is useful; the second is not.

Student Answer A

John Agard is proud of his Caribbean heritage and he resents Britain for belittling his sense of Caribbean identity.

Student Answer B

John Agard was born in Guyana.

Themes

Identity

Agard points out that without a past, in the form of history, we have only an incomplete sense of ourselves: our real identity is obscured.

Compare with
'My Last Duchess': the duke has taken everything from his first wife. The portrait is the identity he has imposed on her.

Power and possession

White Europeans once were the conquerors of most of the world. Agard suggests that not only did they possess the land, they also rewrote the histories of those lands, thus taking possession of the past.

Compare with
'London': the ordinary people have been dispossessed. Everything is 'chartered' (owned) by the rich.

Social conflict

Agard's poem is rebellious and defiant, hinting that if conventional history is not changed, then Afro-Caribbeans and other dispossessed people will change it for themselves and assert their real identities.

Compare with
'Tissue': Dharker wants to see 'daylight break' through the structures built by the proud and powerful.

DOIT!

Choose two more themes relevant to 'Checking Out Me History' and to Power and conflict.

For each theme, list one more poem that you could compare with 'Checking Out Me History'.

Briefly explain each of your choices.

Language

The poem is written phonetically: words are spelled as they would sound when spoken by someone from John Agard's historical and cultural background: for example, 'de' (the), 'bout' (about). The words are not just written phonetically; they are also written in a Caribbean **dialect** rather than in Standard English. For example:

> dem [they] tell me   he [his] cat   what happen[ed] to de Caribs

By writing in non-standard dialect, Agard makes the dramatic monologue more compelling: we can 'hear' the accent of the speaker; we can imagine the lively personality that gives the narrative energy and urgency.

Look at how one student deals with this aspect of the poem:

John Agard makes his narrator strong and defiant: he refuses to conform to 'proper' English and this strengthens his refusal to accept official versions of history. John Agard makes us hear the narrator and this brings him to life for us, making him real and rebellious.

Structure and form

The poem is a dramatic monologue brought to life by the authentic voice and the colourful details. The whole poem is structured like a song that shifts between two moods. The first is the swaggering, sarcastic mood of complaint about the inequality between black and white history. These parts tend to have extended rhyming lines with a bouncing rhythm that support the scornful tone.

The other sections – marked out in italics and indented – use shorter and irregular lines that slow the reading down in respect for the black hero being described.

See how one student refers to details in the poems to support their ideas about another aspect of the poem's structure, repetition:

Repetition of phrases - especially of 'Dem tell me...' - gives a sense of a building threat, something ominous that cannot be resisted. It's like a drum beat that grows in strength right up to the end of the poem. Finally, the narrator reveals the thing that cannot be resisted: his determination to assert ('carve out') his identity by learning about 'me own history'.

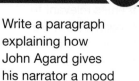

John Agard's narrator is not very complimentary about the white British version of history that he received at school. What language and techniques does he use to convey this view?

STRETCHIT!

Write a paragraph explaining how John Agard gives his narrator a mood of determination. Consider how repetition supports this mood.

REVIEW IT!

1 Translate into Standard English: 'Dem tell me bout'.
2 What can the narrator not see because he cannot see his own history?
3 What does the narrator mean by 'me own history'?
4 Who did Toussaint L'Ouverture beat?
5 Which country's independence was inspired by Toussaint?
6 How are a cat and a fiddle relevant to the poem?
7 Who was Lord Nelson?
8 Where did Mary Seacole come from?
9 Choose one example of rhyme and briefly explain its effect on the meaning of the poem.
10 What is the narrator planning to do at the end of the poem?

DO IT!

- Add your own annotations to the poem, exploring more of its details and their effects. Include the underlined words or phrases.
- Online you will find a copy of the poem with more detailed annotations.

AQA exam-style question

Compare how poets present attitudes to inequality in 'Checking Out Me History' and in one other poem from Power and conflict.

[30 marks]

Shaka memorial

Kamikaze

Beatrice Garland (b.1938)

<u>Her</u> father embarked at sunrise
with a <u>flask of water</u>, a <u>samurai sword</u>
in the cockpit, a <u>shaven head</u>
<u>full of powerful incantations</u>
5   and enough <u>fuel for a one-way</u>
<u>journey into history</u>

but half way there, <u>she</u> thought,
recounting it later to her children,
he must have looked far down
10   at the little fishing boats
<u>strung out like bunting</u>
<u>on a green-blue translucent sea</u>

and beneath them, arcing in swathes
<u>like a huge flag</u> waved first one way
15   then the other in a figure of eight,
the dark shoals of fishes
flashing silver as their <u>bellies</u>
<u>swivelled</u> towards the sun

and remembered how he and
20   his brothers waiting on the shore
built cairns of pearl-grey pebbles
to see whose withstood longest
the turbulent inrush of breakers
bringing their father's boat safe

25   – *yes, grandfather's boat* – safe
to the shore, <u>salt-sodden</u>, <u>awash</u>
<u>with</u> cloud-marked mackerel,
black crabs, feathery prawns,
the loose silver of whitebait and once
30   <u>a tuna, the dark prince, muscular, dangerous.</u>

And though he came back
my mother never spoke again
in his presence, nor did she meet his eyes
and the neighbours too, they treated him
35 *as though he no longer existed,*
only we children still chattered and laughed

till gradually we too learned
to be silent, to live as though
he had never returned, that this
40 *was no longer the father we loved.*
And sometimes, she said, he must have wondered
which had been the better way to die.

Summary

A narrator tells the story they have heard from their mother: how her father once turned back from a wartime suicide mission and was as a result shunned by his family and community forever.

The narrator's grandfather – a pilot – set off on a kamikaze mission in his plane. (His head was 'full of powerful incantations', suggesting he was on a mission that had been filled with religious importance and ritual.)

The narrator's mother *assumed* that her father must have seen all the beauty below him – fish shoals, the 'translucent sea' – and remembered playing on the shore with his brother as children, and this made him change his mind and turn back. (Notice that the poem does not give a definite reason for why the grandfather changed his mind.)

The narrator's grandfather probably recalled his own father returning from the sea with his varied and attractive catch of fish, including – once – a very impressive tuna. (All the details simply given to the reader are very seductive. They are magical and naturally raise the question, why would you kill yourself and lose all that beauty?)

When the grandfather returned home, he was shunned even by his wife. Only his children treated him normally. (The narrator quotes their mother's words here, so that the kamikaze pilot's daughter narrates most of the rest of the poem.)

Eventually the children rejected their father too. His daughter wondered if suicide would have been a better way of dying. (There is a contrast between two sorts of death here: actual death, and social death which might be even worse.)

DEFINE IT!

arcing – curving

cockpit – where a pilot sits in a plane

embarked – set off

incantations – a set of words that often have magical or religious powers

kamikaze – see 'Context' page 81

samurai – Japanese warriors hundreds of years ago, famous for their thin, curved swords

swathe – a wrapping, often made of a large amount of cloth

translucent – something that light can shine through

turbulent – fast and chaotic

Context

Late in 1944, when Japan was losing the war to America, thousands of Japanese pilots began to fly their planes into American ships to terrify and to destroy. These suicide bombers were celebrated as heroes in Japan and came to be known as 'kamikaze' – the wind of God.

NAIL IT!

Any comments you make about context must shed light on the poem *and* the exam question. Look at how one student achieves this double relevance during their answer to the question at the end of this section. An examiner has made some notes alongside.

> Not everyone's experience of conflict is physical, not even a Kamikaze pilot's. Beatrice Garland shows us a man who intends to use himself as a weapon of war but is stopped by conflicts within himself.

The student draws on the broader understanding of conflict, the focus of the *question*.

Understanding of conflict in *this poem*.

Themes

Inner conflict

It seems that the pilot was torn between the suicide mission inspired by 'powerful incantations', and by his desire to live, motivated by the beauty of the seascape and his happy memories.

Compare with
'The Emigrée': the emigrée is torn between her understanding of reality and her feelings for the city she grew up in.

Social conflict

The pilot has a patriotic and social 'duty' to kill himself. When he betrays this sacred duty he is treated as dead by his family and community.

Compare with
'Checking Out Me History': the narrator resists the pressure to conform and to accept his society's 'normal' values.

Regret/guilt

The pilot might or might not regret his decision. Apparently his daughter believes that he must have come to regret his decision – in some ways at least.

Compare with
'War Photographer': the photographer is tormented by memories and feelings connected to his photos.

Give two possible reasons why the kamikaze pilot turned back.

STRETCH IT!

Write a paragraph explaining what Beatrice Garland might want us to think of the pilot's decision to turn back.

Language

The descriptive details in the poem are mostly clear and factual, helping the reader to see them clearly in their mind. The details are so evocative and beautiful that they are almost magical in effect: the 'translucent sea', the fish's 'flashing silver', the 'cloud-marked mackerel'. This form of magic acts on the pilot's mind as a sort of antidote to the dark magic of the 'powerful incantations' that urge him to give his life for his country.

The occasional similes and metaphors move beyond description to suggest the underlying themes of the poem. For example, the simile 'like a huge flag' reminds us of the military mission that the pilot suddenly rejects, choosing life and family over patriotism. The metaphor 'dark prince' emphasises the tuna's strength and danger, as if it represents the punishment that awaits anyone who breaks the rules of routine duty – however extreme these might be, in the case of a kamikaze pilot.

Look at how this student uses evidence to explore the effects of one example of language:

> When their father returned from the mission, at first his children 'chattered and laughed', suggesting their innocence, but eventually they 'too learned to be silent'. The word 'learned' is chilling because it suggests either that the adults 'taught' the children to ignore their father, or that they felt forced to do that to 'the father we loved'.

Structure and form

Complete the table for stanzas 4–7. Summarise the topic of each stanza in no more than eight words.

The poem is in seven stanzas, each the same length. Each stanza acts like a paragraph, dealing with its own topic, so as to guide the reader through the main events and then their significance:

Stanza	Topic
1	Setting off on the kamikaze mission
2	Beauty on the sea
3	Beauty under the sea

The last two lines of the poem are a form of commentary, probably summing up the poem's main point: there is more than one way to die, and actual death can be better than social death.

The story is told by a grandchild of the pilot, who quotes their mother for most of two stanzas, so that the narrative becomes complex and multi-layered.

See how one student explores the *effect* of this layered narrative. An examiner has made some notes alongside.

The story is told by a grandchild, based on what their mother has told them, and they even quote their mother's own narrative for most of the last two stanzas. The mother does not know for certain the reason for her father's change of mind. She can only assume that 'he <u>must have</u>' looked down and seen the beauty below, and that changed his mind. The distance Garland places between the pilot and the reader through this layered narrative means that the reader doesn't feel at one with the pilot and cannot automatically sympathise with his decision. This distancing technique leaves the reader to make up their own mind about what to think.

Recognition of the poet's deliberate choices.

Clear focus on the effect on the reader.

STRETCH IT!

To what extent do you agree with this student's views? Do you agree that Garland deliberately distances the reader from the pilot?

REVIEW IT!

1 When did the pilot take off?

2 Why did he not take enough fuel to get home?

3 What must the pilot have first seen when he was flying over the sea?

4 What must he have seen below the sea's surface?

5 Who would he have remembered waiting with on the shore?

6 What does the word 'feathery' suggest about how the boys might have felt about the prawns?

7 Why was the pilot treated 'as though he no longer existed'?

8 What does 'dark prince, muscular, dangerous' suggest about the boy's memory of the tuna?

9 What lesson does the narrator's mother think the pilot might have learned?

10 Who are we expected to sympathise with most in the poem?

DO IT!

- Add your own annotations to the poem, exploring more of its details and their effects. Include the underlined words or phrases.

- Online you will find a copy of the poem with more detailed annotations.

AQA exam-style question

Compare how poets present ideas about conflict in 'Kamikaze' and in one other poem from Power and conflict.

[30 marks]

Essentials

DO IT!

- Re-read all the poems.

- Note down how each one is relevant to the overall Power and conflict theme.

For example, in 'Ozymandias' we are presented with a picture of a ruined statue abandoned in the desert. This is a monument to the power of Ozymandias – a power so great that he declares himself 'king of kings', all others should 'despair'. However, this monument is a 'colossal wreck', broken and scattered across the 'level sands'. The reader understands that power is vulnerable and fragile. It is an illusion and merely temporary.

DO IT!

Find the poems that use these language features:

- plain, colloquial language

- references to nature

- the creation of vivid and detailed visual images.

Themes

The overall theme for all these poems is Power and conflict. Don't lose sight of that: *power and conflict should be the 'focal point' of your study of all the poems*. The theme is quite broad: not all the poems are about war – or even about heroism or lack of it. Regret and guilt is another clear focus. You see this in poems such as 'London', 'Remains' and 'War Photographer'.

NAIL IT!

Focus on the key element in the question.

Within the overall Power and conflict theme, your exam question will choose a specific key element, such as the power of nature, heroism, control or social conflict.

- Make sure you spot the key element in the question.

- Stay relevant to that key element throughout your answer.

Language

When you re-read the Power and conflict poems, notice any similarities in language style and methods, even if the poems come from different points in history. For example, 'Storm on the Island' uses an extended metaphor of a military attack to show the violence of the breaking storm. In 'Tissue' we see an extended metaphor used to show the power of paper to 'alter things' as we record our history and make records of the past.

Another example of shared language is the use of light imagery to create a sense of positivity and hope. This technique is used in two poems which create a sense of place: 'The Emigrée', where images of sunlight show an idealised childhood memory, while Extract from, 'The Prelude' references light on water, which evokes the tranquillity of the scene where the boy is working positively with nature.

Other shared patterns of language you could explore include: images showing the reality of war and conflict in 'Exposure', 'Bayonet Charge', 'Remains'; images from nature in 'Storm on the Island', Extract from, 'The Prelude', 'Poppies', 'Ozymandias'.

Structure and form

Think about how the structure and form of each poem helps your understanding of meaning and effect. The shape of 'Tissue' is flowing and delicate – as fragile as the paper it describes. The sonnet form of 'Ozymandias' is dense and formal – rather like the grandeur and self-importance of Ozymandias himself. 'Checking Out Me History' has a looser form with varied stanza lengths, but also a structure that suggests folk songs, with a chorus that listeners can join in with.

It is worth reading poems aloud and hearing the rhythms and sounds that give each poem a distinct pattern and coherence. We have already looked at the song-like qualities of one of the poems, but you will find that all the poems have their own distinctive sound. For example, 'The Charge of the Light Brigade' uses repetition of lines, words and sounds to drive the pace of the poem and to create a relentless charge as the rhythm of the poem captures the sound and motion of galloping horses. By contrast, 'My Last Duchess' reads slowly but evenly, the form suggesting the narrator's insane calmness, his confidence, his lethal sense of purpose.

Context

The Power and conflict poems come from different times and cultures; they are written by poets who have different attitudes and beliefs, and have had different personal experiences. Readers have changed too. Social attitudes change throughout history – especially regarding war and conflict. Other examples include: changing attitudes towards warfare from the 19th century until the modern-day 21st century; changing attitudes towards patriotism and duty; and growing awareness of other cultures and identities. This is what we mean by 'context': the circumstances that explain the tone and ideas in a poem.

NAILIT!

By all means, allow what you know of a poem's context to help you to write meaningfully about the key element given to you in your exam question. However, in general the best rule is to let the poem speak for itself: don't read too much into it by trying to make it explain aspects of the poet's life. Focus on *your* reaction to the poem and the methods the poet has used to create that reaction in you.

DOIT!

Look back through all the poems:

- Read them aloud.

- Note down anything distinctive about patterns in them – repeated sounds and techniques.

- Find other poems that are similar in structure and form, and poems that contrast with them.

Read the notes on the structure and form of each poem in the previous pages. These will help you to make your own notes and to compare and contrast poems.

Doing well in your AQA exam

Understanding the question

NAILIT!

- Your AQA exam question will name one Power and conflict poem and tell you to compare it with another Power and conflict poem of your own choice.

- The named poem will be printed on the paper.

- **Read the question before you read the named poem** so that you re-read the poem with the question focus in mind.

- Read the question carefully and understand it. Make sure you stay relevant to the question.

Make sure you understand your exam question so that you do not include in your answer material that is irrelevant to what the question has asked.

Below is an AQA-style question. The question has been prepared by a student so that they fully understand it. Look at their notes.

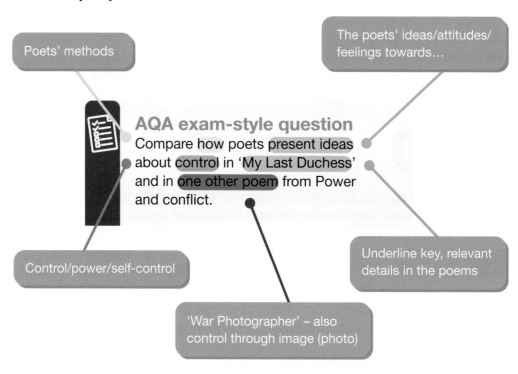

Poets' methods

The poets' ideas/attitudes/feelings towards…

AQA exam-style question
Compare how poets present ideas about control in 'My Last Duchess' and in one other poem from Power and conflict.

Control/power/self-control

Underline key, relevant details in the poems

'War Photographer' – also control through image (photo)

This student has studied the question carefully and decided that:

- the focus is on different sorts/examples of control

- 'ideas about' includes the poets' attitudes and feelings (tone)

- 'War Photographer' is a good choice of comparison/contrast with the named poem.

'Pinning the question down' like this – making sure it is understood properly – will help the student to look out for useful evidence to support their answer. In the examination room it is easy to misread questions, answering the question you hoped to see, rather than the one that is actually on the paper. Once you have prepared the question in the way shown above, you will be ready to re-read the named poem in the light of the question focus. As you read, underline relevant details.

DOIT!

Choose another question from earlier in this *AQA Study Guide*. Prepare the question as above.

Planning your answer

Once you have spent a couple of minutes 'pinning down' the question, planning an answer will be quite straightforward. Your brief plan should set out:

- your key, *relevant* ideas
- the content of each of four or five paragraphs
- the order of the paragraphs.

Practise planning as part of your revision programme.

Here is the same student's plan for their answer to the exam question on page 86:

NAILIT!

Spend 7–10 minutes on understanding the question, reading the named poem and planning your answer. There are no marks for using lots of words. Instead, you should aim to write enough *good*, *useful* words. Aim for four or five well-planned paragraphs (plus a brief introduction and conclusion).

Paragraph	Content		Timing plan
1	Introduction - use the question prep to establish focus of answer and my own choice of poem.		9.35
2	Explore 'My Last Duchess' - evidence of narrator as a controller (of wife and listener).		9.38
3	How the portrait is a form of control	Refer back to question focus/ wording.	9.45
4	'War Photographer': role of pictures as form of (self-) control (cf MLD)		9.52
5	Overall comparison of attitudes: how do the two poets make us feel about the forms of control? 'ordinary pain' (WP); Fake modesty (MLD)	Sometimes consider connotations of 'control'.	9.59
6	Brief conclusion - which poem's picture of control is more shocking for a modern reader?		10.05

Sticking to the plan

Note how this student has jotted down time points when they should move on to the next section of their answer. That way they make sure they do not get stuck on one point and fail to cover the question focus in enough breadth.

Planning to meet the mark scheme

The plan above suggests that the student knows what the examiner is looking for. (See the summary mark scheme on page 88.)

DOIT!

Go back to the exam question which you chose for the Do it! on page 86. Develop a brief plan for it as above.

Assessment Objective (AO)	What the plan promises
AO1 (Read, understand and respond)	Understanding of a number of ideas relevant to the main question focus – control, power and *self*-control. Some personal interpretations to be included – suggested by pictures as a form of control.
AO2 (Language, form and structure)	Exploring the poems will include close engagement with language/form, e.g. tones and how these are carried by details in the poems; effects of language choices ('connotations').
AO3 (Context)	How readers in different times might react differently ('modern reader').

What your AQA examiner is looking for

Your answer will be marked according to a mark scheme based on three assessment objectives (AOs). The AOs focus on specific knowledge, understanding and skills. Together, the AOs are worth 30 marks, so it is important to understand what the examiner is looking out for.

Mark scheme

AQA will mark your answers in 'bands'. These bands roughly equate as follows:

- band 6 approx. grades 8 and 9
- band 5 approx. grades 6 and 7
- band 4 approx. grades 5 and 6
- band 3 approx. grades 3 and 4
- band 2 approx. grades 1 and 2.

Most importantly, the improvement descriptors below will help you understand how to improve your answer and, therefore, gain higher marks. The maximum number of marks for each AO is shown.

Assessment objective (AO)		Improvement descriptors				
		Band 2 Your answer…	**Band 3** Your answer…	**Band 4** Your answer…	**Band 5** Your answer…	**Band 6** Your answer…
AO1 (12 marks)	**Read, understand and respond**	supports simple comparisons between the poem with references to textual details.	sometimes explains comparisons between the poem in relation to the question.	clearly compares the poem in relation to the question.	develops a thoughtful comparison of the poem in relation to the question.	critically explores and compares the poem in relation to the question.
	Use evidence	makes some comments about these references.	refers to details in the poem to back up points.	carefully chooses close references to the poem to back up points.	thoughtfully builds appropriate references into points.	chooses precise details from the poem to make points convincing.
AO2 (12 marks)	**Language, form and structure**	mentions some of poets' methods.	comments on some of the poets' methods, and their effects.	clearly explains poets' key methods, and their effects.	thoughtfully explores poets' methods, and their effects.	analyses poets' methods, and how these influence the reader.
	Subject terminology	uses some subject terminology.	uses some relevant terminology.	helpfully uses varied, relevant terminology.	makes thoughtful use of relevant terminology.	chooses subject terminology to make points precise and convincing.
AO3 (6 marks)	**Contexts**	makes some simple inferences about contexts.	infers poets' points of view and the significance of contexts.	shows a clear appreciation of poets' points of view and the significance of contexts.	explores poets' points of view and the significance of relevant contexts.	makes perceptive and revealing links between the poem and relevant contexts.

AO1 Read, understand and respond/Use evidence

Make sure you read and answer the question carefully. Your examiner will look for evidence that you have answered the question given. Do not go into your exam with an answer in mind. Knowing the poems very well will give you the confidence to show your understanding of them and their ideas as you answer the question on the paper in front of you. You mustn't just show off your knowledge and understanding of the poems: you need to use that knowledge and understanding to answer the question thoughtfully.

Using evidence means supporting your ideas with well-chosen, relevant references to the poems. They can be indirect references – such as brief mentions of an idea or description in a poem – or direct references – quotations. Choose and use evidence carefully so that it really does support a point you are making. Quotations should be as short as possible, and the very best ones are often neatly built into your own writing.

AO2 Language, form and structure/Subject terminology

The language and structural features in a poem have been chosen carefully for effect. Good answers will not just point out good words a poet has used: they will explore the likely effects of those word choices on the reader.

Subject terminology is about choosing your words carefully, using the right words and avoiding vague expressions. It is also about using terminology *helpfully*. For example, here are two different uses of subject terminology in relation to the poem 'London', the first much more useful than the second:

Student answer A

'Marriage hearse' is a shocking oxymoron because it suggests that love causes death, so that there is no possible shelter from the urban misery that Blake describes: the reader understands that even warm emotions are lethal.

Student answer B

'Marriage hearse' is a great oxymoron.

AO3 Contexts

Notice the emphasis on '*relevant* contexts' higher up the mark criteria. Here are some useful questions to hold in your head when you refer to context:

- How might the society a poet lived in have influenced their ideas and attitudes?

- What beliefs and assumptions have influenced how you respond to poems you are writing about?

- How has comparing poems enriched your understanding of them?

The best answers will only include contextual information that is directly relevant to the question, not just the poem.

NAILIT!

To boost your marks when answering questions, do the following:

- Know the poems well. Read and study them. Make up your own mind about them.

- Don't go into the exam with ready-made answers.

- Read the question and make sure you answer it thoughtfully.

- Choose details in the poems that support your points.

- Always comment on the *effect* of details you choose.

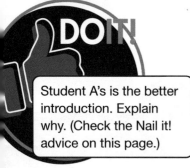

DO IT!

Student A's is the better introduction. Explain why. (Check the Nail it! advice on this page.)

Writing your answer

Getting started

You have looked at one student's plan, and you will have noticed that they have decided to write a short introduction. Here are the openings of two students' answers to the question on page 86: Compare how poets present ideas about control in 'My Last Duchess' and in one other poem from Power and conflict.

Student answer A

Browning's 'My Last Duchess' shows the narrator as a man who wishes to impose his control over everyone around him: the duchess, the listener in the poem and the reader. In 'War Photographer', Carol Ann Duffy also explores control. However, here control is shown as the control of an image and the photographer's self-control.

Student answer B

I am going to write about how two poets write about control. First, I am going to write about 'My Last Duchess', which was published in 1842, then I am going to talk about 'War Photographer', which was published in 1985. This is a long time apart so they will understand control differently. Those are the sorts of things I'm going to write about in my answer.

The response

Look at the student's plan for the essay on page 86. Here is a part of paragraph two of that student's answer. Note the way they use quotations to closely examine relevant details of Browning's language choices. An examiner has made some comments in the margin.

Browning presents the narrator in 'My Last Duchess' as seeking to control both his wife and the listener sent by the Count. The duke immediately controls the situation as he bids the listener, 'Will't please you sit and look at her?' - the imperative 'sit and look at her' being hidden cleverly behind the seemingly courteous 'Will't please you'. He directs the listener to the expression on the Duchess's face in the portrait, telling him - and therefore controlling his viewpoint - about the 'depth and passion' of her look. His control slips slightly when he allows the listener and the reader to glimpse the threat within his nature. The duke says that viewers ask about his dead wife's expression, only 'if they durst', clearly suggesting that the duke is a feared man.	The words of the question are used to clearly focus on what is being asked.
	Direct evidence used – and built neatly into student's own words.
	Confident focus on writer's craft
	Using synonyms for control to keep on track.
	Using words from the question to keep on track.
	Effect of words is identified and analysed closely

Paragraph topics

The rest of your paragraphs should each deal with a subtopic of the main focus of the question. Here, the question focuses on the poets' presentation of ideas about control. The student's plan suggests that the next three paragraph topics will be: an exploration of how the portrait is a form of control in 'My Last Duchess', then how 'War Photographer' explores control through the role of the photographs, then an overall comparison of how the two poets make us feel about the forms of control. The 'overall comparison' paragraph will help the student to address the 'Compare how poets present' aspect of the question: in other words, the student can explore what each poet wanted the reader to learn and understand about control.

Below you will see how – in part of their 'overall comparison' paragraph – the same student makes reference to the poets' attitudes to control, by exploring how the poets make the reader feel about control. This shows that the student understands that the poems are constructed to express ideas or sometimes a definite message. The references are underlined to point them out.

> Both poets present ideas about control but with <u>contrasting attitudes</u>. In 'My Last Duchess,' Browning shows the reader the threat and menace of someone who seeks to control the thoughts and actions of people around them. We see the duke concealing his ruthlessness through vague language. He refers to the orders he gave without being specific about what those orders were and he says 'This grew' without explaining what this refers to. His false modesty alerts the reader to his attempt to conceal his anger about his wife's kindness when he talks of her equal thanks to 'anybody's gift' to his greater gift of his ancient family name.
>
> In 'War Photographer' Duffy presents a narrator who controls the pain he feels within a war zone by controlling images and through distancing himself from the suffering he witnesses. Duffy presents the photographer's self-control as he continually reminds himself that someone must do this job. The reader is presented with a stark contrast between the 'ordinary pain' that we are faced with that can be dispelled simply by good 'weather' and the photographer's self-control as he takes images of 'A hundred agonies'.

Ending your answer

Don't worry about elaborate conclusions: if you have nothing more to say, then just stop. The answer we have been looking at just ends like this:

> Both poets show how control is a part of our lives and has been part of our lives throughout history. A modern reader understands the need to control our emotions and reactions to events to protect ourselves, as we see in 'War Photographer'. However, the modern reader will be shocked by the control the duke seems to have placed on his late wife and the control he seeks to exert over the listener's thoughts.

NAILIT!

Key rules for writing a good answer:

- Understand and plan.
- Be aware of the mark scheme (see page 88).
- Answer the question, making clear and relevant points.
- Back up your points with evidence, including some short quotations.

Using evidence:

This student uses indirect evidence to make general references to ideas in the poem and uses direct evidence in the form of quotations when they know them. Both forms of evidence are valid.

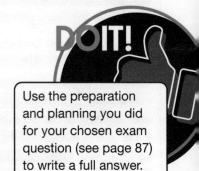

DOIT!

Use the preparation and planning you did for your chosen exam question (see page 87) to write a full answer.

Going for the top grades

Of course you will always try to write the best answer possible, but if you are aiming for the top grades then it is vital to be clear about what examiners will be looking out for. The best answers will tend to:

• show a clear understanding of both the poems and the exam question • show insight into the poems and the question focus • explore the poems in relation to the focus of the question • choose evidence precisely and use it fluently	AO1
• analyse the writer's methods and their effect • use relevant, helpful subject terminology	AO2
• explore aspects of context that are relevant to the poems and question.	AO3

A great answer **will not** waste words or use evidence for its own sake.

A great answer **will** show that you are engaging directly and thoughtfully with the poems and the question, not just scribbling down everything you have been told about the poems.

The best answers will be RIPE with ideas and engagement:

R	• Relevant	Stay strictly relevant to the question.
I	• Insightful	Develop relevant insights into the poem, its structure and themes.
P	• Precise	Choose and use evidence precisely so that it strengthens your points.
E	• Exploratory	Explore relevant aspects of the poems, looking at them from more than one angle.

DO IT!

Find an essay or practice answer you have written about Power and conflict.

Use the advice and examples on this page to help you decide how your writing could be improved.

Below is a small part of a student's answer to the question about how poets present ideas about control in 'My Last Duchess' and 'War Photographer'. An examiner has made notes alongside.

What strikes me about Duffy's presentation of the photographer's self-control in the face of the evidence gathered in his 'spools of suffering' is that despite his impassive 'stare' as he moves to his next assignment, there is admiration for his intentions. Duffy shows her anger, not towards the photographer, but instead towards the editor who is controlling what we see through the selection of 'five or six' images and the public who 'do not care'. Duffy's message here is about the way our culture consumes these images but is immune to the suffering they show. The photographer is unable to control people's reactions to the images.

The duke in 'My Last Duchess' shows us a bleak and damaged view of control. He tries to control and manipulate the emotions of his mysterious listener with his hesitant speech, denying his power as an orator, 'which I have not', suggesting that he is an unconfident, humble man instead of a cruel tyrant. His bitterness towards his late wife is evident as he relates what aspects of her behaviour 'disgusts' him. He presents this as normal behaviour, using a question to manipulate the listener into agreement as he asks, 'Who'd stoop to blame/this sort of trifling?' This manipulation of the listener and control of the Duchess is instantly recognisable for a modern reader. His need to control and the sense of threat this produces creates a chilling and menacing narrative.

Clear and **nuanced** points.

Precise evidence neatly integrated into the argument.

Control explored here.

Precise choice of evidence

Original insight based on context

Good return to question focus to maintain relevance.

REVIEW IT!

1 In your exam, how long should you give yourself to prepare, plan and write your Power and conflict answer?

2 What are the other two sections in Paper 2?

3 How long should you spend planning and preparing your Power and conflict answer?

4 Why is it important to prepare or 'pin down' your exam question?

5 If you are in the examination and you find that you can't remember any direct quotations from your chosen poem, what can you do?

6 How many marks are AO1, AO2 and AO3 worth together?

7 Your friend has told you that they are going to learn an essay that they wrote in the mock exams as their revision. What would you say?

8 'Introductions and conclusions are not essential.' Is this true or false?

9 Create your own question by filling in the blanks:
Compare how poets present _____ in _____ and in one other poem from Power and conflict.

10 Plan a five-paragraph response to the question you created in question 9.

NAILIT!

In the month leading up to the exam, all your revision should be based on planning and writing answers to exam questions. You will find plenty of exam questions in this guide for practice.

Glossary

alliteration Starting words that are close to each other with the same sound (for example: 'wrings with wrong').

allusion An indirect reference to something; a reference that is implied, but not made explicitly (for example: the 'valley of Death' in 'The Charge of the Light Brigade' alludes to the Bible's 'valley of the shadow of death').

blank verse Poetry that does not **rhyme**.

caesura In poetry, a pause near the middle of a line.

colloquial Informal language that is appropriate for speech but not usually for writing.

connotation An implied meaning (for example: the duke's strong hint ('I gave commands') that he has had his wife murdered in 'The Last Duchess').

context (contextual) The circumstances in which a poem was written or is read. These could include the personal experiences of the poet, or the typical attitudes of a modern reader.

dactylic rhythm A **metre** (**rhythm**) made up of dactyls: in a dactyl, a **stressed** syllable is followed by two unstressed syllables (for example: 'cannon to right of them,/Cannon to left of them…' in 'The Charge of the Light Brigade').

dialect The conventions that apply to how someone writes or speaks in order for them to make sense. Saying 'me history' rather than 'my history' in 'Checking Out Me History' is a matter of dialect: in Standard English it is wrong; in some other dialects it is normal. 'Checking Out Me History' is written in a Caribbean immigrant dialect rather than in Standard English.

effect The impact that a writer's words have on a reader: the mood, feeling or reaction the words create in the reader.

enjambment Continuing the sense of one line on to the next one. Usually a writer does this by not using punctuation at the end of a line (for example: 'whose frown/And wrinkled lip,…' in 'Ozymandias').

euphemism The deliberate choice of a mild word or phrase to soften a harsh or shocking idea (for example: 'passed away' instead of 'died'; 'trifling' instead of 'offensive behaviour' in 'My Last Duchess').

extended metaphor A **metaphor** that is reworked and developed in a poem (for example: images relating to storms in 'The Charge of the Light Brigade').

iambic A type of **rhythm** which follows a pattern alternating between an unstressed and a **stressed** syllable (for example: 'The bough of cherries some officious fool' in 'My Last Duchess'). Each pair of unstressed and stressed syllables is an iamb.

iambic pentameter A line of poetry made up of five iambs. (See **iambic** above). The line therefore has ten syllables with a **stress** on the second, fourth, sixth, eighth and tenth syllables (see example in **iambic** above).

imagery Pictures in words. The main forms of imagery (other than description) are **similes** and **metaphors**.

infer Work something out by using clues and hints. We have to infer information that is only implied rather than being explicit (for example, in 'My Last Duchess' we infer that the duke has killed his wife).

metaphor Comparing two things by saying they are the same for effect (for example: 'exploding' waves in 'Storm on the Island' – the waves are not literally exploding).

metre The **rhythm** in a line of poetry, created by the regular stressing of syllables. Many poems do not have a set metre.

monologue A speech. A 'dramatic monologue' is a poem in which the **narrator** tells a story (for example: 'My Last Duchess').

narrator The person (character) who tells the story in a poem or in fiction. Usually we accept the narrator's version of events. Sometimes – for dramatic effect – a writer creates a narrator we cannot trust: an unreliable narrator.

nuance Slight and subtle differences in shades of meaning.

onomatopoeia When a word makes a sound similar to what is named (for example, 'cuckoo', 'gurgle' or the 'smack' of bullets in 'Bayonet Charge').

oxymoron Two normally contradictory words combined for effect (for example: 'marriage hearse' in 'London').

personification Treating a thing as though it is alive (for example: 'the jaws of Death', as though death is a living thing and has jaws. Here Death is personified with a capital D as though it is a name, and as ferocious and devouring).

rhyme A line whose last **stressed** syllable has the same sound as a nearby line ending (for example: 'rows'/'glows' in 'War Photographer'. If the stressed syllable is not the last syllable in a line, then any following syllables must rhyme too (for example: *biscuit/risk it*).

rhyming couplet Two lines in a row that **rhyme** together.

rhythm The 'beat' of a line of poetry. Rhythm comes from the way the **stresses** (or 'beats') 'fall', or, more likely, are placed by the poet. If the stresses fall at regular intervals, we say that the line has a 'regular rhythm'.

sibilance A sound effect in which 's' sounds are repeated in words close to each other (for example: 'sabre-stroke' in 'The Charge of the Light Brigade'; 'through the silent water stole my way' to suggest the swish of oars in Extract from, 'The Prelude').

simile Comparing two things using 'like' or 'as' (for example: 'like a tame cat/Turned savage' in 'Storm on the Island'; 'numb as a smashed arm' in 'Bayonet Charge').

stanza Another word for 'verse'. 'Verse' is normally used for songs, 'stanza' for poetry.

stress Emphasis that falls on certain syllables to create a beat or **rhythm**.

structure The way a poem is organised so that it is coherent. The structure of a poem is its shape, its patterns of **imagery**, the sequence of its ideas.

verb A doing, being or having word (for example, to walk, to be or to have). Verbs change their form to show present (*walk*), past (*walked*) or future (*will walk*).

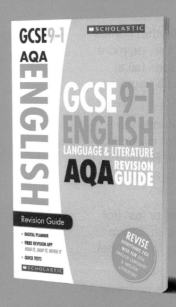